Tomkin
In the Staffordshire Moorlands

A history of hamlet and chapel

© Irene Turner 2006

ISBN 0-9544080-7-X

Three Counties Publishing (Books) Ltd
P.O. Box 435, Leek, Staffordshire, England, ST13 5TB

Printed by PhotoPrint of Leek - Tel: 01538 384482

Introduction

"The Little Chapel in the Moorlands" is held dear in many people's hearts. It has survived closure on a number of occasions and been saved each time by the commitment and will-power by the local community.

In 2004, my Great Aunt, Joan Willshaw and I were discussing the Chapel and the plans that members had for it. Their aim was two fold. The first to develop the Chapel by building an extension to provide a meeting room, kitchen and toilet facilities and also provide running water. Secondly their aim was to become part of a Hidden Britain project. Hidden Britain is an initiative which encourages visitors into lesser know parts of the countryside, and therefore the Chapel would become multifunctional, by providing refreshments, tourist information, local history etc to these visitors and also serve the spiritual needs of the local community at other times. Therefore ensuring the survival of the Chapel for generations to come.

This conversation with my Great Aunt and also one regarding a local history day that they had held at the Chapel led to the start of this book. At first I thought that it would not take too long, why Tomkin was only a little hamlet, little did I know that it would take over a year to research, gather material and write up.

Any profit made from this book will go to the Tomkin Chapel Mission development fund. The Project needs **£38,000**. If you too feel that you would like to help the Tomkin Chapel project by offering a donation please send a cheque payable to Tomkin Chapel, to Mrs Joan Willshaw, Treasurer, Tomkin United Reformed Chapel, I Dalehouse Road, Cheddleton, Nr. Leek, Staffs, ST13 7JL.

Acknowledgements

Many thanks to those who shared their photographs and memories with me, these include: - Miss Mary Allsopp, Mr James Bailey, Mrs Cynthia Brammer, Mr Tommy Charlesworth, Mr Arthur Docksey, Mr Peter Handley, Mr and Mrs David and Nora Landon, Mrs Jean McNicol, Mr Geoff Perkin, Mr and Mrs Rogers, Mrs Ivy Simcock, Mrs Edith Steele, Mrs Jean Turner, Mrs Freda Unwin, Mrs Joan and Fred Willshaw, and Mrs Bette Wilson.

A thank you also goes to The County Record Office, The Sentinel, the Leek Post and Times newspapers and the State Library of South Australia for permission to use relevant articles and photographs, and Matthew Wilson for proof reading.

Contents

Chapter One

Location of Tomkin

Tomkin is situated in both the Staffordshire Moorlands villages of Bagnall and Cheddleton. The boundary line passing through what was once "The Smithy".

Tomkin historically was part in the ancient parish of Bucknall-cum-Bagnall and part in the Parish of Cheddleton. Both parishes being in Totmonslow Hundred; a former administrative area comprising of four market towns, about eighty townships, consisting of ten chapelries and thirty parishes.

Tomkin/Bagnall was also in the Manor of Horton. The Manor included Horton parish, Rushton James, Endon, Longsdon and Stanley. In 1796 the manor was sold to Thomas Harding whose son eventually sold it to Edward Antrobus in 1808, by 1834 Lord of the manor was G. C. Antrobus, Esq. of Eaton Hall, Cheshire. The Manor stayed with the Antrobus family until 1926 when manors virtually came to an end with the passing of the Law of Property Acts.

The Lordship for the Manor of Cheddleton in 1851 was Thomas Powys who had inherited the title from his brother Edward. The title was then passed to Catherine his sister (Mrs Ansdell), and when she died in 1870 the manor was sold.

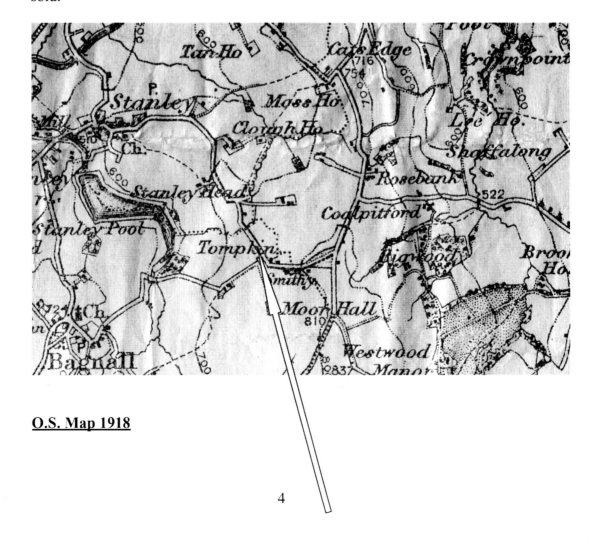

O.S. Map 1918

Chapter Two

Legend of Tomkin

Tomkin has long been associated with Bonnie Prince Charlie and the Scottish Rebellion of 1745. The legend being that Tomkin gained its name from a Scottish drummer named Tammas. (Thomas-Tom).

"The event is said to have taken place in the winter of 1745 when kilted Scots came down with Bonnie Prince Charlie, and arrived in Staffordshire early December.

William Augustus, Duke of Cumberland (1721-1765), British army commander and son of George II was in the area waiting for them with a large army.

The story goes that Bonnie Prince Charlie and his officers stayed uninvited at Bagnall Hall, the home of Squire Murhall. They ransacked his house after subjecting him to various humiliations and then fled.

Tammas the drummer was left behind because he had drunk too much elderberry wine. He was captured and imprisoned in the dungeons at Moor Hall Farm. Somehow he escaped, only to be captured on Knowsley Common. The furious Squire appeared on the scene and ordered him to be flayed, saying: "I'll have a drum made from his broad back".

His skin was sent to Endon Tanneries to be made into a drum. However, word quickly spread that it could not be treated by the normal tanning process. Mother Critchlow, the local midwife, and her son Rafe, stole the skin at the dead of night, and buried it on top of the body.

So Tom's skin became Tomkin and a spring at the spot is said never to have run dry".
Source: unknown

The following article is another version of the legend written and researched by W.M. Jamieson.

"Whilst on their way to Leek, a group of the Pretender's highland troops was spreading terror as they ravaged south living off the land as they went. A party of the invaders billeted themselves at the home of Squire Murhall for a few days before moving on and rampaging their way to Leek. When they had gone, the Squire angered by their presence and incensed at the damage caused to his home sought revenge. He seized an unfortunate wounded Highland straggler and wreaked a terrible vengeance. According to the legend, the soldier, a 15 year old drummer boy named Tam, was flayed alive with the intention of making a drum from his skin.

Although there is little doubt that the incident is factual, the conflicting stories which later grew from the affair are now part of the mythology of the Leek area. The most popular story related how the skin proved impossible to tan into leather despite all the skills of the local tannery at Endon. In desperation the skin was buried in a field near Endon and where houses were later built on. The place was called Tam's Skin, a name which eventually corrupted to Tomkin.

Story tellers with a more vivid imagination tell of a successful tanning of the skin and making of a drum which hung for a time in Saint Luke's Church, Endon. The drum must have found great disfavour in the house of God for soon there were reported mysterious calamities in the area; crop failures and mysterious cattle deaths. It was not long before the ghost stories were being told and locals were circumspect about venturing abroad in the dark. Some of these ghost stories have persisted and motorists have alleged the ghost of a highland drummer on the Leek Road.

Squire Murhall suffered a terrible revenge for his deed at the hands of retreating highland troops who avenged their former comrade by beating his killer into an insensibility from which he awakened to a lifetime as a permanent cripple.
Source: Murders, Myths and Monuments of North Staffordshire, W.M. Jamieson.

The event has been talked about for many years and is recorded has far back as 1829. Simeon Shaw who wrote the "History of the Staffordshire Potteries" in 1829 talks to several people including a William Willett, of Eaves, (Eaves is in the parish of Bucknall-cum-Bagnall , 3miles east of Hanley) he reports that *"William Willett who died 8th September1827 aged 105 *, well remembered Mr. Murhall, of Bagnall, skinning one of the sick Rebels left there, and endeavouring to get the skin dressed as leather; for which, on the return of his comrades from derby, they emasculated Mr Murhall between Biddulph and Congleton; and for which he never after was known to enjoy a comfortable day."*

John Ward stated that the legend is unquestionably true. John Ward wrote "A History of the Borough of Stoke-on-Trent" (1843), also quotes a letter from a Mr James Middleton (brother to Rev. John Middleton curate of Hanley). James Middleton was commissioned to make observations on the rebel forces. The following is an extract from the letter to a friend in London.

Shelton 28 Dec 1745
"Sir, as to the *Rabels* you were speaking of they were no further than Derby, and returned back to Leek on Saturday, the 15th inst,, and made very bad work; but as to 500 of them laying down at Wigan was false. I was at Whitmore with Esq. Manwairing the day before Christmas-day, and he told me he had taken about 100 of them, and killed about 30, and they had killed about ten of ours; and we look every day when the duke overtakes the whole body of them. Will Hassells and brother Parson were taken prisoners by them at Leek, but were released the next day following. About 30 with their horse came to Bagnall, and took Justice Murhall along with them, and kept him two or three days; it's said he gave them £300 to be released". The letter continued with other matters and ends,
I am your sincere friend, James Middleton

John Ward also recounts the following discussion between Ralph Leigh and John Telwright in Burslem in 1810, it was originally written in old North Staffordshire or Moorland dialect and is one of other subjects discussed on this day, the following relates to the legend and a translation follows:-

Burslem 1810
The conversation starts with Telwright asking Ralph Leigh his age, Leigh replies 82, and a little later John Telwright stating that he himself was only 5 or 6 at the time of the 1745 rebellion.

Leigh. 'The young Pretender with his officers stayed to breakfast at the Squires (William Murhall of Bagnall Hall), and afterwards the Scotch soldiers robbed his house of his fire arms and money, and made him show them the road toward Derby'.

Telwright. 'But they found their way back again pretty soon afore the duke could meet with them?'

Leigh. 'They did and the Squire thought he would make amends for robbing his house; so he caught a lazy Scotch rogue as had lagged behind, - tucked him up with a halter (a rope to hang criminals) over a sign post at Leek, had him flayed like a calf, and sent his hide to the tan yard to make into leather for a drum-head'.

Percy W. L Adams who wrote the "History of the Adams family" in 1914, stated that there was a firmly held tradition that Prince Charles received hospitality from William Adams, gentleman of Bank House, Bagnall (he was a Potter as well as a Farmer of his estate) staying for one night early in December in that year, while a number of his followers ravaged the home of the Murhall's near by. A teapot in salt-glaze, made by John Adams of the Brick House Pottery, is said to have been used on the occasion at breakfast and was for a long time treasured by the family.

This legend has often been disputed so the following evidence has been gathered in support:-

Ralph Critchlow married at St Edward's Church, Leek 6th October 1725 and was buried 15th February 1777.

Shaw states that **William Willett** died 8th September 1827 and was buried at Endon. He was in fact buried at Endon but the correct burial date was 12 June 1827 and he was aged 104, abode given as Eaves Farm. It is more likely that the 8th September was his birth date and that he was in his 105th year. Shaw stated that Willett was born in the eighth year of the reign of George I. George I became King in 1714 so William would have been born in 1722. Parish records again were checked and a William Willet was baptised on the 24 October 1722 at Leek Parish Church, son of Jason and Mary Willet.

Ralph Leigh stated that he was 82 in 1810. Ralph was buried at Burslem on 2 November 1814 aged 85. He would have been born circa 1728/29 and would have been about 16 or 17 in 1745 - a good age to remember such events.

John Telwright stated he was only 5 or 6 in 1745 so again parish records were searched and on the 2 March 1740 a John Telwright son of Samuel and Jane Telwright was baptised at Burslem parish church.

All those mentioned did exist.

Besides the above information other authors have written on the 1745 Rebellion, Christopher Duffy wrote "The '45 – Bonnie Prince Charlie and the untold story of the Jacobite rising" who provides the following extracts that seem to support that it was possible:-

Leek 3ʳᵈ December
"All along as they have travelled they take all the horses, saddles, bridles, boots, armour or anything else they can carry off…. They ill-used many people, particularly Mr Lockett, whom they tied neck and heels, because he would not discover where his son was, who by his diligence had given them great offence"

Leek 7ᵗʰ December
"There was a fretful, snappish feeling among the troops, who shot 3 local men in or near Ashbourne, as well as the landlord of the Hanging Bridge Inn on the way to Leek.

Successive parties looted Okeover Hall, and there was further plundering in Leek itself; Lord George noted that his great difficulty was "to bring up stragglers, who could not be kept from going into houses and committing abuses".

Leek 8ᵗʰ December
"Out to the west a party of cavalry marauded in the villages between Leek and Newcastle under Lyme, which produced a powerful but altogether unintended diversion".

Chevalier de Johnstone who's "Memoirs of the rebellion in 1745 and 1746", contains a narrative of the progress of the rebellion from its commencement to the battle of Culloden quotes "our stragglers seldom failed to be attacked by the English peasants".

Finally an extract from James Ray's "History of the Rebellion" (1754). James Ray was a volunteer under his Royal Highness the Duke of Cumberland wrote the following:-

December 8. "On the Duke's arrival at Cheadle, in Staffordshire, the country people brought in a rebel spy, which they delivered to our army, when on their march to Macclesfield, where he was hanged on a gibbet, and ordered to hang until 8 o'clock at night, when about that time Mr G   A-------an Apothecary and surgeon, in this town, went to the Centinel to buy the body, which he bought for 4s.6d. the Dragoon who sold it thought it a good price, and the Doctor likewise well pleased with his bargain; intended to anatomize his carcass, and expected to have had leather of the skin, (worth his money) which he accordingly gave to the tanner to dress, but the miracle mongers say, that the hide was so holy a nature, that it would not tan, nor be confined to lye under water, by any weight that could be put upon it, so that the tanner after much labour lost was obliged to take this holy hide and bury it".

A very similar story and supporting evidence that such events did happen.

William Murhall

The Murhall family lived at Bagnall Hall for hundreds of years. William was born circa 1676 it is known that he married Lydia and had 2 children Dorothy and Thomas circa 1718-19. Lydia died in 1725 the service took place at St Peter and St. Vincula in Stoke on the 21 May 1725.

Thomas is recorded in the Cambridge University Alumni. He entered Christ's College, Cambridge in 1738; records state he was the son of William, born at Bucknall, Staffs, who attended school at of Mr Slade at Dilhorne. During his life he was Vicar and died 1784 buried 21 March, at Moulton, in Suffolk.

William was appointed High Sheriff of Staffordshire 2nd February 1742.

Dorothy married John Adams 25 August 1747. Soon after his daughter Dorothy married in 1747, it is reported that the Murhall family migrated to Moreton Say Hall, Salop. Bagnall Hall was rebuilt again in 1777 by William's descendent John Murhall.

William Murhall is buried at Endon Church, where the monument to his memory has the following inscription:

Beneath lie the remains of William Murhall, Esq., late of Bagnall, who died 4 January 1762, aged 66

Part of what I possessed is left to others and what I gave away remains with me

Chapter Three

History of Tomkin

It has been suggested that Tomkin could be a derivative of the surname of Tomkinson i.e. son of Tomkin. The Tomkinson family of Endon were known to have been in the area as far back as the 1600's. There were Tomkinson's residing in Cheddleton in the 1600's; the will of a Thomas Tomkinson of Cheddleton was proved in Oct 1669.

There are references to people named Tomkin in the Cheddleton Parish Registers for example William Tompkins was buried 4 June 1706, Thomas Tomkin was buried 20 November 1751 and John Tomkin married Elizabeth Bagnall 12 May 1734, and there was also a Josias Tomkin.

The Will of Josias Tomkin was proved in the year 1719/20. Josias lived at 'Laund' in the parish of Cheddleton. Laund is now known as Lawn Farm, located on Park Lane, Endon, and is very close to the present Cheddleton/Endon border, but not near enough to Tomkin to say that an ancestor or descendent of gave their name to the area concerned.

Hence the legend lives on.

Tomkin, Tompkin or Tomskin

The spelling of Tomkin differs at times, so some documents may refer to Tomkin and others as Tompkin. There is nothing unique in this, there are many other documented cases where locations and even surnames were spelt and written how the words sounded.

Maps of 1815 and 1816 both state Tomkin, the enumerator of the 1861 Census spelt it as Tomkin, and the locals too spelt it as Tomkin as far back as 1870 which can be seen from Chapel memorial inscriptions.

The enumerator who undertook the 1841 and 1851 Census, and various other historical ordnance survey maps refer to the little Hamlet as Tompkin.

In 1881 and 1891 the Census enumerator reached the little Hamlet and wrote in his ledger "TOMSKIN".

Earliest recorded mention of Tomkin

The first documented mention of Tomkin is found on a map of Staffordshire dated 1775.

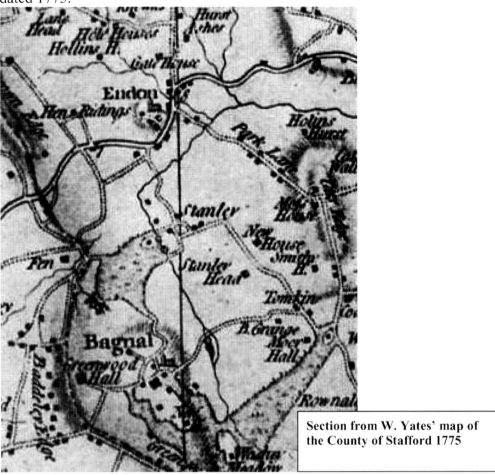

Section from W. Yates' map of the County of Stafford 1775

The next mention of Tomkin was found in a will of the late William Heath dated 26 March 1793. William Heath was a Yeoman farmer and living in Tomkin at the time of his death. The will was proved at Lichfield 1 May 1800.

Tomkin 1816

Bagnall was at one time in the Manor or Horton. A survey undertaken in 1816 for Sir Edward Antrobus (Baronet) identifies who owned or occupied land in the Manor.

This survey reveals that Hugh Ford, Thomas Hammersley, William Turner, Francis and John Hargreaves and John Grindey lived and worked in the centre of Tomkin at this time, although it did not necessarily mean that they owned the land which can be seen from the map and entries made in the accompanying ledger.

Survey of the Manor of Horton
Comprising the Parish of Horton and several townships of Endon, Longsdon and Stanley in the Parish of Leek and the township of Bagnall in the parish of Stoke upon Trent in the County of Staffordshire 1816
Image reproduced by courtesy of the Staffordshire Record Office D(W)1909/E/9/1

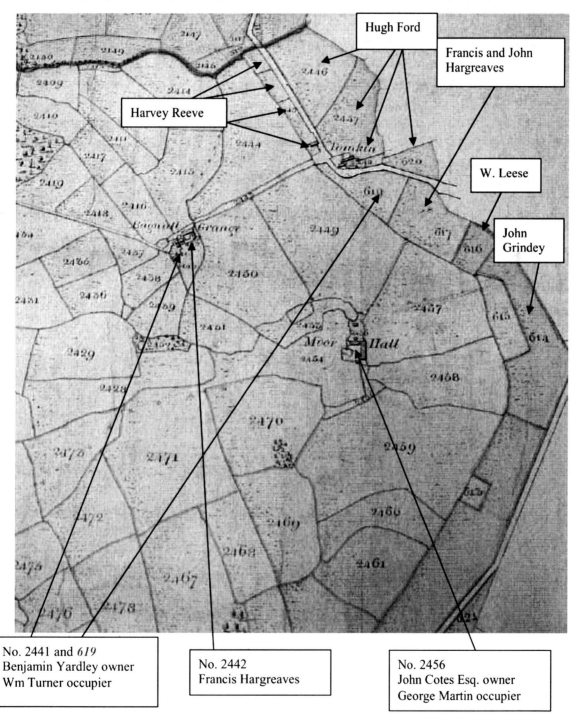

Hugh Ford

Francis and John Hargreaves

Harvey Reeve

W. Leese

John Grindey

No. 2441 and *619*
Benjamin Yardley owner
Wm Turner occupier

No. 2442
Francis Hargreaves

No. 2456
John Cotes Esq. owner
George Martin occupier

Entries from ledger:-
A = Acres, R= Roods, P= Perches

Yardley, Benjamin Owner	Wm Turner Occupier			A	R	P
		2422	Flint Mills	1	2	9
		2431	Pool Head	3	1	20
		2432	Do	1	.	24
		2433	Do	1	2	12
		2434	Lane Close	5	2	21
		2435	Middle Field	2	.	34
		2436	Do	2	.	11
		2437	Near Home Close	1	.	35
		2438	Middle Do.	1	2	34
		2439	Far Do.	1	3	37
		2441	Homestead (Bagnall Grange)	.	.	34
		2497	Mill Dam	.	2	17
			Sub total	23	1	3
		619	Allotment	2	.	34
			Total A . R. P.	25	1	37

It can be seen that Benjamin Yardley owned over 25 acres and the Homestead (2441) property is Bagnall Grange, but it should also be noted that other property number (2442) again called Bagnall Grange on the map was owned by Francis Hargreaves.

Hargreaves, Francis	In hand	2409	Forge Field	2	1	31
		2410	Black Croft	2	1	22
		2411	Long Meadow	2	.	.
		2412	Broad Meadow	4	1	24
		2413	Lane	.	1	6
		2414	Holly Tree Field	5	.	8
		2415	Pin Field	4	3	25
		2416	Back House Meadow	2	1	30
		2417	Little House Meadow	1	3	6
		2418	Little Lime Kiln Fields	1	3	20
		2419	Lime kiln field	2	2	27
		2440	Hemp butt	.	3	12
		2442	Homestead (Bagnall Grange)	.	.	39
			Sub total	31	1	10
		617	Allotment	3	2	38
			Total A.R.P.	35	.	8

Francis Hargreaves, (his brother John was not recorded at this stage) owned just over 35 acres. 617 is the plot of land which was sold to William Turner in 1817.

Ford, Hugh Owner	In hand	2446	Far Field	5	.	1
		2447	Near Field	4	1	12
		2448	Homestead	.	2	14
			Sub total	9	3	27
		620	Allotment	1	1	11
			Total A.R.P.	11	.	38

Hugh Ford owned just over 11 acres. Plot number 2448, the Homestead, was in the centre of Tomkin.   It is understood that this is where Tomkin Head Farm is today.

Hammersley Thomas Owner	Reeve, Harvey	2445	House, Garden and 3 Crofts	1	2	30
			Total A.R.P.	1	2	30

Harvey Reeve rented just over 1 acre from Thomas Hammersley. This area of land is where Lane End Farm is located today

Moor Hall Farm

John Cotes Esq	George Martin					
		2420	Cliff and Lane	5	2	18
		2426	Pool Head		3	8
		2443	Heath Lane		2	24
		2444	Lower Heath	8	2	2
		2449	Big Heath	11	3	2
		2450	Little Heath	8	-	29
		2451	New Meadow	2	2	7
		2453	Cord Hay croft	1	3	14
		2454	Home Field	5	3	21
		2455	Lane		2	25
		2456	Homestead		2	27
		2457	White Fields	9	2	10
		2458	Cloy Hall	5	3	25
		2459	Big Cow Hay		14	35
		2460	Coopers Meadow	3	2	22
		2461	Far Fields	4	3	19
		2462	Far Fields		5	15
		2643	Gorsy Bank	4	2	3
		2464	White Field Meadow	6	1	11
		2465	Birch Coppice			
		2666	Patch	10	2	29
		2467	Stone Wall Piece			
		2468	Turnip Piece	3	1	32
		2469	Little Stock Flatt	5	-	-
		2470	Big Stock Flatt	7	-	10
		2471	Barn Field	10	-	18
		2472	Little Gorsy Knowl	4	-	5
		2473	Upper Black Flatt	4	-	33
		2474	Lower Black Flatt	5	3	31
		2478	Lower Gorsy Knowl	5	3	38
		2479	Little Brook Field	5	-	12
		2480	Big Brook Field	5	-	33
		2481	Far Laund Piece	7	-	2
		2482	Near Laund Piece	9	-	3
	Total			184	-	4

John Cotes was the owner of Moor Hall in 1816. The 184 acre land was rented by George Martin and family.

Tomkin Between 1831 and 1838

Thomas and Anne Basnett were living/farming at Tomkin in 1831, their son Alfred was baptised at Bagnall Church in June of that year. By 1841 they had moved.

James and Mary Davenport were also known to be living in Tomkin between 1835 and 1838 from information taken from the Bagnall Parish Registers, James is stated as being a labourer, and by 1841 the family had moved.

The other main sources of references are taken from 1841-1901 census material. This material gives us a 'snap shot' of information about the families who lived in Tomkin on one night every ten years.

Moor Hall and the Smithy are the only two properties which are easy to identify from this material; and these are described in more detail later. The other properties are not so easy to identify, and therefore are left to the reader to work out who was living at which property, whether it is Tomkin Head Cottage, Tomkin Head Farm or Lane End Farm.

1841

The 1841 Census named 4 main families living in Tomkin. These families being William and Ann Salt, Samuel and Elizabeth Wood(s) Ralph and Ann Knight and Hugh Ford and his sister Ellen Heath along with their children and servants.

William and Ann Salt
Very little is know about William and Ann Salt other than he was a farmer, by 1851 they had moved away.

Ralph and Ann Knight
Ralph Knight was married to Ann with 2 children, Frances and James, Ralph was an agricultural labourer, again others were living here but it is impossible to decipher some of the information and again relationships are unknown. By 1851 the family had moved.

1851

The 1851 Census again names 4 households in Tomkin. These being William and Hannah Brooks, Thomas Heath (Jnr.) and his sister Mary, Samuel and Elizabeth Wood and Ellen Heath with her married daughter Ellen Simcock.

William and Hannah Brooks
William Brooks was married to Hannah with 2 children, Phoeby and William. He was a farmer of 13 acres and also worked as a farm labourer. By 1861 they had moved. It is known that in 1871 that the Brooks family were living at Stanley Moor with children Hannah, Anne and George. William now owned 9 acres of land and also worked as a Railway labourer.

18

Thomas and Mary Heath (Brother and Sister)

Thomas and Mary are the children of Thomas and Ellen Heath of Moor Hall and Caverswall. Thomas was baptised 6 June 1830 and Mary 30 July 1828 both at Caverswall.

In 1851 Thomas and Mary appear on the Census as farming an 85 acre farm at Tomkin, employing one indoor and one outdoor servant.

1861

The 1861 Census names Samuel and Elizabeth Wood, Ellen Heath, and two new families Martha Billinge, and Samuel and Julia Fenton.

Martha Billinge

Martha lived with her 3 children at Little Tomkin she was a widow and worked as a schoolmistress.

More information can be found about Martha Billinge in the section on Chapel memorial inscriptions.

Ellen Heath

By this time Ellen had now left Moor Hall, living at the same property was her daughter Ann, son Thomas, and her brother Thomas Ford, now a retired farmer.

1871

The 1871 Census names James and Jane Wood, Ralph and Olive Alcock, Joseph and Sarah James and John and Eve Sherratt.

Ralph and Olive Alcock

Ralph Alcock was born in Onecote and Olive in Cheddleton; they now farmed 57 acres, with the help of their 3 children.

Joseph and Sarah James

Joseph and Sarah were both originally from Kingsley. Joseph was a coalminer.

1881

The 1881 Census names William and Fanny Deakin, Ralph and Olive Alcock, Tm. Henry and Sarah Durose and Daniel and Sarah Steele.

Ralph and Olive Alcock

Ralph and Olive were still resident but by 1891 they had left.

Thomas Henry and Sarah Durose

Thomas H Durose was born in London, he was married to Sarah, farming 3 acres, Thomas also worked as a labourer locally. Sarah's Mother also lived with them at this time. By 1891 they had moved to Cellarhead Road, Cheddleton, with 2 of their children and Sarah's mother. Thomas was now working as a paper maker.

1891

The 1891 Census names William and Fanny Deakin, William and Ellen Chell, Isaac and Annie Simcock and Daniel and Sarah Steel(e).

William and Ellen Chell

William and Ellen lived and farmed in Tomskin. In 1891 they had 6 children ranging from 10 years old to 5 weeks old. By 1901 they had moved to Fernyhill, Cheddleton with 7 of their children.

Isaac and Annie Simcock

Isaac and Annie lived and farmed at Little Tomskin, both originally came from Horton. By 1901 they were no longer resident in Tomkin.

1901

By 1901 four new families had moved into the area; William and Sarah Perkin at the Smithy, Joshua and Annie Steele at Moor Hall and those mentioned below:-

Joseph and Eliza Shenton

Joseph was a Forge Labourer who was born at Withy Stakes, Cheddleton, and his wife Eliza was born at Baddeley Edge. They appeared to have moved to Tomkin around 1887.

John and May Banks

John was also a Forge Labourer originally from Clayton, his wife May from Armshead, Werrington. John continued to live here until at least 1939.

James and Sarah Myatt

James Myatt was a Farmer born in Bagnall, he and his family appear to have moved to Tomkin around 1900. By 1901 James and Sarah Myatt had 4 children and by 1918 the family had moved.

Chapter Four

Moor Hall Farm

Moor Hall dates back to the sixteenth century and was a moated farmhouse.

It is identified on W. Yates' Map of the County of Stafford in 1775.

The Martin family were known to have lived at Moor Hall, information from two headstones in Cheddleton Churchyard reveal that William died in 1813 aged 39, John Martin died in 1819 aged 82 and Mary his wife 1813 aged 76, were all from Moor Hall. It would appear that they were the father and Grand Parents of George who was named as tenant there by 1816.

George Martin married Hannah Walker 27 October 1812 by Licence at Cheddleton Church. They had a number of children who were baptised at Bagnall Church; entries of these can be found at the back of the book. It would appear that they moved away by the early 1830's when it is known that the Heath family had moved in by 1833. George Martin died in 1837.

By 1841 the farm had new tenants or owners, being Hugh Ford and his sisters Ellen Heath.

Moor Hall – 1841 Hugh Ford and Ellen Heath (brother and sister)

Hugh Ford was baptised 19 December 1790 at Norton in the Moors, son of Hugh and Catherine. Hugh never appears to have married and by 1816 owned 11 acres of land in Tomkin, by 1841 he was living at Moor Hall with his widowed sister Ellen Heath and her daughter Catherine along with 7 servants. Hugh was described as a farmer and land owner.

Hugh died in 1841, his will was proved 29 April 1842, he left his real and personal estate to his sister Ellen Heath for her natural life and at her decease the estate was to be sold and divided equally between the Ellen's children, with the exception of a legacy of £100 to his nephew Thomas. He also wished that the tenants rights of the farms which he held to pass to Thomas (on the death of his sister Ellen) if the landlords were agreeable.

Ellen Ford was baptised at Norton in the Moors 30 June 1801, she married Thomas Heath and it is known that they lived in Tomkin in 1821 as records show that Ellen their daughter was baptised at Bagnall Church in January of that year. They then appeared to have moved to Caverswall as subsequent children were baptised at Caverswall Church.

Thomas (Snr) died 21 January 1833 and is buried at Caverswall. His headstone states "Thomas Heath of Moor Hall".

By 1851 Ellen is now head of the household at Moor Hall, a widow and described as a "landed proprietor". Her daughter Ellen had married and was now Ellen Simcock. By 1861 Ellen had now left Moor Hall, but still living in

Tomkin with her daughter and son, Ann and Thomas, and her older brother Thomas Ford, a retired Farmer, along with 3 servants.

By 1861 **Samuel and Julia Fenton** had moved to Moor Hall.
Samuel was born circa 1800 and Julia circa 1804. In 1851 they were farming a 55 acre farm at Sneyd Green. By 1861 they were farming Moor Hall, Samuel described as a farmer of 127 acres. They lived at Tomkin for a short time with 5 of their children, Sarah, Ralph, Ephraim, Harriet and Alice. They also employed a Cowman and Ploughman. Julia died in 1865 and by 1871 Samuel had retired and went to live with his son at Bucknall.

By 1871 **John and Eve Sherratt** had now taken over Moor Hall. John originally from Congleton and Eve from Biddulph farmed the 126 acres with 3 of their sons. By 1881 Eve had died and John and his son John had retired and had moved back to Congleton.

By 1881 **Daniel and Sarah Steel(e) (Brother and Sister)** were farming Moor Hall. Daniel was born circa 1840, he farmed Moor Hall, and his sister Sarah acted as Housekeeper. At this time their brother Ephraim, his wife and daughter were staying with them as Ephraim was out of work.

Daniel and Sarah Steel (Brother and Sister) are still living and farming at Moor Hall 10 years later in 1891. Their widowed Mother was also living with them. By 1901 they had moved to farm at Luzlow in Bagnall where Mrs Steele was now described as head of the household living with Daniel and Sarah.

By 1901 Joshua and Annie Steele were now farming and living at Moor Hall. Joshua being brother to Daniel.

From 1918 Moor Hall was farmed by **Edgar and Alice Docksey** and has been farmed by the Docksey family since that time.

Moor Hall Circa 1920 Edgar Docksey with horses

Moor Hall Circa 1952-56 – Tractor driving the thrashing machine
Mr Brassington top left, owner of the thrashing machine, Albert Docksey bottom left and
Edgar Docksey with sack

**Moor Hall Farm is associated with the rebellion of 1745, when it is said that Squire
Murhall imprisoned the Scottish drummer in the cellar. The full story of this legend can be
found in Chapter One. The cellar was filled in some years ago to enable structural changes
to be made to the farmhouse.**

Arthur and Albert Docksey Circa 1950's – Cellar at Moor Hall prior to be filled in

Chapter Five

The Smithy, Tomkin

1841 - Samuel and Elizabeth Wood

Samuel Wood was married to Elizabeth with 2 children at home at this time. Samuel was the village Blacksmith. There are others listed but the records were hard to decipher and also on the 1841 Census relationships were not stated so it is hard to establish what relation others in the household were to Samuel.

1851 - Samuel and Elizabeth Wood

Samuel and Elizabeth continue to live and work in Tomkin 10 years later. Samuel is now a Master Blacksmith and farmer of 10 acres.

1861 -Samuel and Elizabeth Wood

Samuel and Elizabeth are still at Tomkin 20 years later, with two of their children. Samuel died in 1870, being Blacksmith at Tomkin for nearly 30 years.

1871 - James and Jane Wood

The Smithy had now passed on to James, son of the late Samuel. James had married Jane and they had 3 children. Elizabeth his Mother lived with them. James employed one man as a Blacksmiths apprentice. By 1881 James and Jane had moved to Fegg Hayes, James working as an Iron Worker.

1881 - William and Fanny Deakin

The Smithy had by this time change hands to William Deakin. William was married to Fanny with one child.

1891 - William and Fanny Deakin

William and Fanny were still resident at the Smithy 10 years later, along with their 4 children. By 1901 the family had moved to Rock End Farm, Wetley Rocks, where it appears that William had given up the work of a Blacksmith to concentrate on farming.

1901- William and Sarah Perkin

William Perkin was born in Kingsley circa 1867, the son of Charles and Elizabeth. By 1881 William aged 14 was a Blacksmiths apprentice. He married Sarah Leese in 1890. Sarah Leese was born in Hanley about 1866, the daughter of John and Sarah Leese. John was a wheelwright.

In 1891 William and Sarah were living at 26 Eaves Lane, Bucknall, he was described as a Blacksmith. By 1900 William and Sarah had moved to Tomkin Smithy.

The Perkin family – The Smithy, Tomkin 1900- 1935

**Hilda, Charles, William (Father) Mabel at back, May,
Sarah Ellen (Mother) and William Jnr Perkin circa 1903
Taken in front of the house at the Smithy, Tomkin**

**Charles Perkin and his father William outside the Smithy at Tomkin with the pony circa
1908**

Sarah Leese, Mabel Perkin, Alby Leese with cap Alf Leese Snr with pipe and Alf Leese Jnr in front. Others unknown. The Leese family visiting Tomkin date unknown.

Hilda, William, Sarah, Charles, May and Mabel Perkin at the back of Smithy House, Tomkin circa 1910

Charles Perkin hot fitting shoes and William Perkin with horse at Tomkin circ 1910

William Perkin with his apprentice at the Smithy, Tomkin – Calendar reveals the month and year to be May 1912

Wedding photograph of Hilda Perkin of Tomkin Smithy to Percy Glover taken 11 June 1922 in the orchard above Tomkin Chapel

Back row left to right:-
Jessie Bloor (Bridesmaid), Bridegrooms brother/ best man, Percy Glover, Hilda Perkin, Charles Perkin (Brides Brother).
Front row left to right: - Parents, Mr and Mrs George Glover and Mrs and Mrs William Perkin.

Mrs Sarah Perkin at Tomkin

Memories of the Perkin family by Geoff Perkin

My Grandparents William and Sarah Ellen (nee Leese) came from Bucknall to Tomkin Smithy around 1900 with their son Charles, who was born and baptised at Kingsley. Their subsequent children William, Mabel, Hilda and May were born at Tomkin, another child, a girl, who I believe was still-born is buried in the grave yard at Tomkin Chapel.

The Perkin family became caretakers at the Chapel, I remember going to a Harvest Festival evening service when I was about 5 or 6 years old, and can remember the smell of the produce in the chapel, and to me in my imagination the place seemed as big as Westminster Abbey.

William farmed the small holding, gathering hay and keeping milking cows, they also kept hens. William had a pony and trap, the pony was a mare, and she bred several foals.

They made butter, and separated cream from the milk with a Diabolo separator which was turned by hand.

Charles started to work with his father on leaving Bagnall School. William was very keen to improve his knowledge of farriery and together father and son became involved with the Staffordshire County Council Farriery classes which were held at the Rodbaston Farm Institute, Penkridge.

In 1912, Charles took over Endon Smithy from Edensor Gibson, his father paid £100 for the ingoing. Charles cycled to Endon from Tomkin each day and after working for 12 months paid his father his £100 loan (interest free) bought a new suit, and was left with 2/6 half a crown (12½).

One day a tramp called at the Smithy, he had raging toothache; he said "Blacksmith, will you take my tooth out? William had removed teeth from cows and horses, so the tramp sat on the anvil block wrapped his arms round the anvil bick, he said "go on blacksmith, pull" and out came the tooth.

Bagnall Parish Council decided to "Beat the Bounds" i.e. following the parish boundary. The boundary between Bagnall and Cheddleton passes right through the Smithy House, so a ladder was placed to allow a man to pass over the house roof. William soon bellowed for him to come down when tiles began to clatter down.

They used to carry out "Firing the anvil". There are square holes in an anvil which are used to handle it when it is being forged. The anvil was tilted up with its bick, or pointed end facing up at an angle, the hole was filled with gunpowder, and a square wooden plug was hammered into the hole very tightly, a small hole was drilled through the plug into the powder, and a small amount of powder was put into that hole, that powder was then ignited and after a short wait, the explosion was louder than any modern firework.

One Saturday afternoon, Charles returned home from Endon Smithy, his father was busy in the garden, he showed Charles a coin he had found, Charles gave him five shillings for it, it was a George III half guinea, and I still have it in my keeping today.

Across the Smithy yard was a small house, the family living there were named Worthington and they had a son, Georgie, as he was referred to by the Perkin family.

Visiting preachers were entertained to tea after the afternoon service, by the Perkin family. I remember William Marson in particular, he was a local preacher and had some amount of control over the Chapel, and he was also an agent for the Royal Insurance Company. I remember a green and red metal advert plate which was fixed inside the back door of Smithy House, bearing the Royal Insurance Company name.

The gents' toilet at the chapel consisted of a wooden cubicle/sort of screen at the rear, the heads or hats of those using it were visible to the lads who were in the field, who used sticks to knock their hats off, before fleeing the owner's wrath.

There is a small well or spring just below and opposite the chapel, enclosed by a semi-circular wall to prevent fouling by horses and cattle which used to pass along the road at that time, this was pure water and the area was kept clean and tidy by those who used it.

Above the Smithy was an allotment garden where vegetables were grown, it was very fertile. The Banks family lived just above this allotment, Mr. Banks tended the stock on his small holding etc and also worked in either Whitfield or Bellerton colliery, he walked both ways, morning and night, people in Stanley village spoke of his clogs resounding on Stanley Bank.

William Myatt farmed just below the Chapel, he and William Perkin became good friends, mutually helping each other in hay making etc, their children became firm friends and I am pleased to say that their grandsons still carry on this wonderful friendship today.

Chapter Six
Electoral Registers- sample entries

Electoral Registers, although not has detailed at the Census material, still gives an insight of who was living in and around the centre of Tomkin. Tomkin being in two parishes made it necessary to consult both Bagnall and Cheddleton registers, many names appeared in both registers.

1902- Bagnall/ Cheddleton

Banks, John	Knowsley
Goodall, Charles	Tomkin
Myatt, James	Tomkin
Perkins, William	Smithy, Tomkin
Steele, Daniel	Moor Hall
Steele, Joshua	Moor Hall

1907/1908-Bagnall/Cheddleton

Alcock, John	Tomkin
Banks, John Snr and Jnr	Knowsley
Deakin, John J	Knowsley
Myatt, James	Tomkin
Perkins, William	Tomkin
Steele, Joshua	Moor Hall

Registers not available between 1909-1917.

1918/1919-Bagnall/Cheddleton

Ball, Edward	Tomkin
Ball, Mary	Tomkin
Banks, John	Knowsley
Banks, Susannah	Knowsley
Bates, Beatrice Lillian	Tomkin
Bates, Reginald	Tomkin
Cope, Edith	Knowsley
Cope, Henry	Knowsley
Docksey, Alice	Moor Hall
Docksey, Edgar	Moor Hall
Handley, Joseph	Tomkin Farm
Handley, Sarah Hannah	Tomkin Farm
Handley, Reubin J	Tomkin Farm (absent)
Perkins, William	Tomkin
Perkins, Ellen	Tomkin
Perkins, Charles	Tomkin
Perkins, William	Tomkin

1923-Bagnall/Cheddleton

Ball, Edward	Tomkin
Ball, Mary	Tomkin
Banks, John	Knowsley
Banks, Susannah	Knowsley
Cope, Emma	Knowsley
Cope, Henry	Knowsley
Docksey, Alice	Moor Hall
Docksey, Edgar	Moor Hall
Leech, Martha	Tomkin
Perkins, William	The Smithy, Tomkin

Plant, Fanny	Knowsley
Weaver, Sarah Jane	Tomkin Farm
Weaver, William J	Tomkin Farm
Weaver, Henry	Tomkin Farm

1928/1929 – Bagnall/Cheddleton

Alcock, Albert	Tomkin
Alcock, Ellen	Tomkin
Banks, John	Knowsley
Banks, Susannah	Knowsley
Banks, Susannah Jnr.	Knowsley
Charton, Susannah	Knowsley
Cope, Henry	Knowsley
Docksey, Alice	Moor Hall
Docksey, Edgar	Moor Hall
Leech, Martha	Tomkin
Gibson, Allan	Knowsley
Gibson, Maria	Knowsley
Perkins, Ellen	Smithy, Tomkin
Perkins, William	Smithy, Tomkin
Weaver, Sarah Jane	Tomkin Farm
Weaver, William J	Tomkin Farm
Weaver, Henry	Tomkin Farm

1933 Bagnall/Cheddleton

Adams, Ethel R	Knowsley
Adams, John Snr	Knowsley
Adams, John Henry	Knowsley
Banks, John	Knowsley
Banks, Susannah	Knowsley
Banks, Susannah Jnr	Knowsley
Docksey, Alice	Moor Hall
Docksey, Edgar	Moor Hall
Gibson, Allan	Knowsley
Gibson, Maria	Knowsley
Gratton, Ernest	Tomkin Head Farm
Gratton, Ernest	Tomkin Head Farm
Gratton, Frederick	Tomkin Head Farm
Gratton, Joseph A	Tomkin Head Farm
Gratton, Lilian	Tomkin Head Farm
Perkins, Ellen	Tomkin
Perkins, May	Tomkin
Perkin, William	The Smithy, Tomkin
Slaney, Ellen	Tomkin
Worthington, Thomas	Knowsley

1939-Bagnall/Cheddleton

Adams, Ethel R	Knowsley
Adams, John	Knowsley
Adams, John Henry	Knowsley
Bailey, Ellen	Tomkin Farm
Bailey, James	Tomkin Farm
Banks, John	Knowsley
Banks, Susannah	Knowsley
Banks, Susannah	Knowsley
Cornes, Hilda	Knowsley Farm
Cornes, Phillip E	Knowsley Farm
Docksey, Alice	Moor Hall
Docksey, Edgar (Snr)	Moor Hall
Docksey, Edgar (Jnr)	Moor Hall

Gratton, Ernest A	Tomkin
Gratton, Megan	Tomkin
Salt, Marion	Tomkin
Salt, Arthur	Tomkin
Thorley, Emma	Tomkin

1945- Bagnall/Cheddleton

Alcock, Harold	The Cottage, Knowsley
Alcock, Hilda	The Cottage, Knowsley
Bailey, Ann Helen	Tomkin Head Farm
Bailey, James	Tomkin Head Farm
Banks, Susannah	Knowsley, Tomkin
Banks, Susannah Jnr	Knowsley, Tomkin
Docksey, Edgar	Wood Lane Farm, Tomkin
Docksey, Mary J	Wood Lane Farm, Tomkin
Docksey, Albert	Moor Hall Farm
Docksey, Alice	Moor Hall Farm
Docksey, Edgar	Moor Hall Farm
Docksey, Reginald	Tomkins Farm
Landon, Charles	Lane End Farm, Tomkin
Landon, Lydia A	Lane End Farm, Tomkin
Proctor, Benjamin	Knowsley Farm
Proctor, Elsie	
Worthington, John	Tomkin Head Farm

1950-Bagnall/Cheddleton

Alcock, Harold	The Cottage, Knowsley
Alcock, Hilda	The Cottage, Knowsley
Bailey, Ann Helen	Tompkin Head Farm
Bailey, James	Tompkin Head Farm
Banks, Susannah	Knowsley, Tomkin
Banks, Susannah Jnr.	Knowsley, Tomkin
Docksey, Edgar	Wood Lane Farm, Tomkin
Docksey, Mary J	Wood Lane Farm, Tomkin
Docksey, Albert	Moor Hall
Docksey, Arthur	Moor Hall
Docksey, Edgar	Moor Hall
Docksey, Reginald	Tomkins Farm
Landon, Charles	Lane End Farm, Tomkin
Landon, Lydia	Lane End Farm, Tomkin
Proctor, Benjamin	Knowsley Farm
Proctor, Elsie	Knowsley Farm
Riley, Alice	Tompkin Smithy Farm
Riley, Hannah	Tompkin Smithy Farm
Riley, James	Tompkin Smithy Farm
Riley, Joseph	Tompkin Smithy Farm
Worthington, John	Tomkin Head Farm

1955-Bagnall/Cheddleton

Bailey, Ann H	Tomkin Head Farm
Bailey, James	Tomkin Head Farm
Banks, Susannah	Knowsley, Tomkin
Banks, Susannah Jnr.	Knowsley, Tomkin
Docksey, Edgar	Wood Lane Farm, Tomkin
Docksey, Mary J	Wood Lane Farm, Tomkin
Docksey, Albert	Moor Hall
Docksey, Arthur	Moor Hall
Findlow, Herbert	Knowsley Farm
Findlow, Lucy	Knowsley Farm
Keeling, Clara	Little Knowsley Farm
Keeling, William	Little Knowsley Farm
Landon, Charles	Lane End Farm, Tomkin
Landon, Lydia	Lane End Farm, Tomkin
Proctor, Mary H	Tomkin Head Farm
Riley, Alice	Tompkin Smithy Farm
Riley, Hannah	Tompkin Smithy Farm
Riley, James	Tompkin Smithy Farm

1960-Bagnall/Cheddleton

Bailey, Ann H	Tomkin Head Farm
Bailey, Ellen K	Tomkin Head Farm
Bailey, James	Tomkin Head Farm
Banks, Susannah	Knowsley, Tomkin
Bennison, Elsie M	Wood Lane Farm, Tomkin
Bennison, Noel E	Wood Lane Farm, Tomkin
Bloor, Edensor	Knowsley, Tomkin
Docksey, Albert	Moor Hall
Findlow, Herbert	Knowsley Farm
Findlow, Lucy	Knowsley Farm
Keeling, Clara	Little Knowsley Farm
Keeling, William	Little Knowsley Farm
Landon, Charles	Lane End Farm, Tomkin
Landon, Lydia	Lane End Farm, Tomkin
Landon, John	Lane End Farm, Tomkin
Landon, Jean E	Lane End Farm, Tomkin
Proctor, George H	Tomkin Head Farm
Proctor, Mary	Tomkin Head Farm
Riley, Alice	Smithy Farm, Tomkin
Riley, James	Smithy Farm, Tomkin

1965-Bagnall/Cheddleton

Bailey, Ann	Tomkin Head Farm
Bailey, James	Tomkin Head Farm
Banks, Susannah	Knowsley, Tomkin
Bennison, Elsie M	Wood Lane Farm, Tomkin
Bennison, Noel E	Wood Lane Farm, Tomkin
Bloor, Edensor	Knowsley, Tomkin
Docksey, Albert	Moor Hall Farm
Findlow, Herbert	Knowsley Farm
Findlow, Lucy	Knowsley Farm
Keeling, Clara	Little Knowsley Farm
Keeling, William	Little Knowsley Farm
Murphy, Ellen	Tomkin Farm, Lane End
Murphy, Wilfred	Tomkin Farm, Lane End
Riley, Alice	Smithy Farm, Tomkin
Riley, James	Smithy Farm, Tomkin
Whilock, Reginald T	Tompkin Smith House

1967-Bagnall/Cheddleton

Bailey, Ann	Tomkin Head Farm
Bailey, James	Tomkin Head Farm
Bailey, Helen	Grange View, Tompkin
Bailey, James	Grange View, Tompkin
Bennison, Elsie M	Wood Lane Farm, Tomkin
Bennison, Noel E	Wood Lane Farm, Tomkin
Bennison, Michael	Wood Lane Farm, Tomkin
Bloor, Edensor	Knowsley, Tomkin
Bloor, Susannah	Knowsley, Tomkin
Docksey, Albert	Moor Hall Farm
Findlow, Herbert	Knowsley Farm
Findlow, Lucy	Knowsley Farm
Keeling, Clara	Little Knowsley Farm
McNicol, Jean	Tomkin Head Cottage
Mountford, John	Little Knowsley Farm
Murphy, Ellen	Tomkin Farm, Lane End
Murphy, Wilfred	Tomkin Farm, Lane End
Whilock, Joan	Smith House, Tompkin
Whilock, Reginald	Smith House, Tompkin

Chapter Seven
Bad winters

This is the lane to Tomkin taken on a Saturday afternoon in January 1955, the Lay Preacher, Miss Nora Birkin, from Chesterton Church, still managed to walk up the lane and turn up on time at Tomkin Chapel for the Sunday Service. Taken by Mrs Sneyd (member of Tomkin Congregation)

Alan Docksey, Tomkin Lane- 1963

Looking up the road to Tomkin - 1963

**Grange View and Tomkin Head Farm with village children
Nicola Allsopp, Gillian Bailey and Andrew Allsopp-1979**

Chapter Eight

Historic archaeological find – 1964

A Bronze Age axe-head was found at Tomkin by Mr Arthur Docksey, one of two brothers who farmed Moor Hall.

It was estimated to be of the early Bronze Age (2,000 B.C.) and found in the bed of a stream at Moor Hall Farm, Tomkin. The prehistoric implement measured about 8" in length and had an hourglass perforation set near the butt. Mr Arnold Mountford, Curator of the Museum went to the farm to inspect the relic and record the exact location of the find. (SJ.942505). It was presented to the Stoke-on-Trent Museum, Hanley and is still in the collection today.

The axe-head was reported by the Leek Post (20 August 1964) to be in perfect condition.

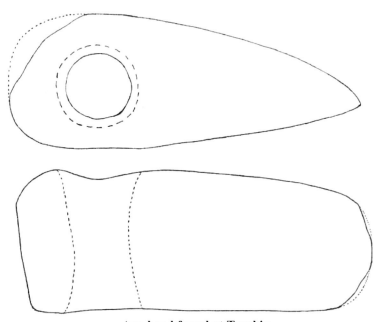

Axe-head found at Tomkin
Mr A. R. Mountford - report of the Stoke on Trent Museum Archaeological Society of 1964.

Chapter Nine
History of Tomkin Chapel

Purchase of land from William Turner

Reverend Newland became Minister at Hanley Tabernacle Church and was there from 1816-1839. He was one of the most notable ministers at this time. He appears to have been an enthusiastic and energetic man, never tiring in spreading Congregationalism over the northern part of the county, and raising capital to open new churches. With his help, Tomkin was one of 14 congregational churches established between 1825 and 1850.

His first attempt to bring religion to the local area was in 1829. When Reverend Newland wrote to the Bishop of Lichfield requesting that a dwelling house could be used as a place of worship.

The Right Reverend the Lord Bishop of Lichfield

I do hereby certify his Lordship that a certain dwelling house situated at Thorney Edge in the Parish of Cheddleton in the County of Stafford and now in the occupation of Richard Bailey is intended to be used as a place of public worship by a congregation of protestants and I request the same may be registered according to the law in this case provided.

Hanley
December 16th 1829

Signed by RW Newland
Minister of the Gospel Hanley
Richard Bailey

This letter can be found in the Minutes of the Tabernacle Independent Chapel (later Congregational Church, Hanley).

Mr Newland had been the main drive for getting a chapel built at Wetley Rocks, near Cheddleton. A Chapel was built but unfortunately did not prove to be a success, and eventually the chapel closed and was then sold. All was not lost though, from the proceeds of this sale, land was bought at Tomkin in 1837.

On the 1st June 1837 fifteen men signed their names to an Indenture. (An indenture is a type of property Deed).The document included the names and parties involved, the price paid and formal words for transferring ownership, it also included a description of the land/property and named current occupier and also those in adjacent properties, it also states on what basis the land/property is sold e.g "fee simple" means that the land is freehold and not on a lease basis. There are also several promises on how the land/property should be used.

The parties involved were as follows:-

Current owner:

William Turner of Bagnall Grange in the parish of Stoke–on-Trent, Wheelwright

Purchasers/Trustees:

1. Reverend Ridgeway William Newland of Hanley in the same parish, Minister of the Gospel

Reverend Newland Circa 1830
Photograph courtesy of the State
Library of South Australia, SLSA: B13649

Reverend Ridgeway William Newland qualified at the Hoxon Academy. Hoxon Academy in London was a training establishment for dissenting ministers founded 1782. He married Sophia by 1820 and who died 6 November 1825. He married Martha his second wife about 1826, there were children from both marriages.

The Reverend Newland left for Australia in 1838/9 taking with him a company of his fellow townsmen, the majority of whom were members of the Tabernacle, he settled on the shores of Encounter Bay. The first substantial building the colonists erected in their new home was a chapel, which they named the Tabernacle. His eldest son, Simpson, became a member of the South Australian parliament.

2. Reverend Samuel Jones of Hanley in the same parish, Minister of the Gospel
Born circa 1813 in Manchester, he studied at the Blackburn Academy, he was Minister at Caroline Street Church, Longton (Independent Church) from 1835-1873. He was married to Mahala. For many years he was secretary to the North Staffordshire Congregational Union he died in 1873.

*3. **Reverend Samuel Barton Schofield** of Burslem in the same parish, Minister of the Gospel*
Born in 1807, Samuel studied at Blackburn Independent College, and at Ashton, Lancashire. He arrived in Burslem in July 1833; he became pastor of the Congregational chapel in Nile Street, Burslem. He was ordained on 27 August 1833 and served as a pastor for 34 years. He married Mary by about 1834; he had two daughters, Margaret and Mary. A new chapel and school were built in 1837 in Queen Street, and thanks to Rev. Schofield's fund-raising efforts the debt was almost negligible by 1866. He died in 1868.

*4. **William Sadler Kennedy** of Burslem aforesaid Engraver*
William began in business in King Street, Burslem, producing palettes for artists in 1838. He moved to Bourne's Bank where he operated Washington Works from 1847-54, being joined by his brother-in-law James MacIntyre in 1852. The factory made door furniture and handles. He lived in Camoys Terrace, Burslem in 1851. He was a member of the Burslem Board of Health 1850-3 and chief bailiff 1849-54. In 1854 he left for London.

*5. **John King Knight** of Fenton in the said parish of S.O.T. manufacturer of Earthenware*
John K Knight was born at Thringstone, Leicestershire, in 1788/9. He married Elizabeth Elkin at Bucknall on 25th January 1813, and had two children, John King Wood and Hannah. He was the chief bailiff for Great Fenton in 1841. He worked the Foley Potteries in Fenton in partnership with the Elkin brothers and John Bridgewood. He was joined by Henry Wileman of London in 1853 who continued alone after John K Knight retired in 1856. He lived at Golden Hill in 1851, and is listed in that year as potter, coal master and farmer of 220 acres. He died at Golden Hill on 15th Mary 1856.

The other Trustees
Very little information could be found regarding the remaining Trustees other than the information supplied within the Indenture.

It is obvious that all were keen to help spread the word of congregationalism and were willing to offer their full support to other ventures in the County besides their immediate home location.

*6. **Benjamin Finney** of Consall in the parish of Cheddleton in the same County, Farmer*
*7. **Samuel Davall** of Blakaley Lane in the parish of Kingsley in the same County, Farmer*
*8. **John Wilson** of Newcastle-Under-Lyme in the said County of Stafford, Accountant*
*9. **Charles Jones**, Druggist of Hanley*
*10. **Samuel Burton**, Earthenware manufacturer of Hanley*
*11. **John Burton**, Earthenware Manufacturer of Hanley*
*12. **William Thornicroft**, Ironfounder of Hanley*
*13. **Matthew Moorhouse**, Surgeon of Hanley*
*14. **Thomas Hill**, Clothier of Hanley*
*15. **John Rowley**, Grocer of Hanley*

The signatures of the above:-

Price paid

Nineteen pounds and twelve shilling sterling

Previous ownership

Previous owners John Hargreaves, forgeman and Francis Hargreaves, Collier, were awarded the land during enclosure of Wetley Moor.

The enclosure award was approved by Parliament in the 48th year of the reign of His Majesty George III, (1808). Enclosure involved fencing of land previously either waste or part of large open fields farmed in strips this was done in order to permit more intensive and profitable cultivation.

An Act for inclosing Lands in the Manor of Horton, in the County of Stafford

"Whereas there are within the Manor of Horton, in which are situate the Parish of Horton, and the several Townships of Endon, Longsdon, and Stanley, in the Parish of Leek, and the Township of Bagnall, in the Parish of Stoke-upon-Trent, all in the County of Stafford, certain Commons and Waste Grounds, containing in the whole, by estimation, one thousand six hundred acres, or thereabouts:

And whereas Edmund Antrobus, Esquire, is Lord of the said Manor, and as such is owner of the soil of the said Commons and Waste grounds, and of all Mines and Minerals within and under the same, and is also Patron of the Perpetual Curacy of Horton:

And whereas the said Edmund Antrobus, the Most Honourable George Granville Leveson Marquis of the County of Stafford, the Right Honourable George Earl of Macclesfield, Sir Thomas Fletcher, Baronet, John Sparrow, William Sneyd, John Fowler, John Hawarth, Thomas Mills, Michael Daintry, William Deebank Hand, John David, Ralph Stevenson, and several other Persons, are Proprietors of and interested in the said Commons and Waste Grounds:

And whereas an Act was passed in the Forty-first Year of the Reign of His present Majesty King George the Third".

Thomas Rowley was appointed commissioner for setting and dividing and allotting the commons and waste grounds within the said Manor between and amongst the Lord thereof and the several proprietors of Estates within the Manor.

Under this act, the land was then given to John Hargreaves and Francis Hargreaves (devise in right of a freehold and titheable estate called Bagnall Grange). Plan VII No. 617, consisting of Three acres, two roods and thirty eight perches on Wetley Moor, bounded northeastwardly by the Tomkin Road and the Parish of Cheddleton, Southeastwardly by the allotment No. 616 and northwestwardly by the allotment No. 619.

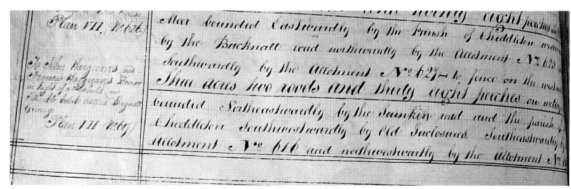

Image reproduced courtesy of the Staffordshire Record Office Q/RDc/69

Extract from enclosure map of 1815.
Plan VII Wetley Moor and Taylors Edge in the Manor of Horton 1815.
Plot 617 – Land sold to William Turner in 1817. The Map also indicates that there was a well located on the land. .

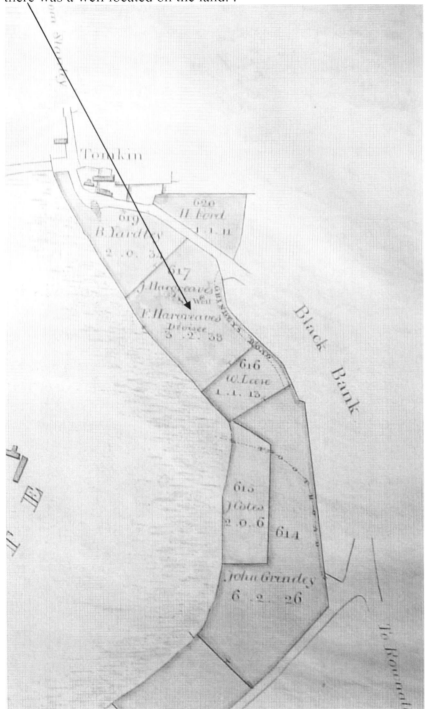

Image reproduced courtesy of the Staffordshire Record Office Q/RDc/69

John and Francis Hargreaves then sold some or the entire plot to William Turner 6th February 1817 (George Hubbard, Gentleman, being Trustee for William).

William Turner sold only part of the plot to the Trustees of Tomkin Chapel.

Conditions of Sale

"Fee simple" (land is Freehold)

Description of land
Situated, lying and being in a place formerly called Wetley Moor with the Manor of Horton and the Township of Bagnall, Stoke-on-Trent, Stafford. The plot is bounded northwardly by the Highway leading from Rose Bank to Stanley, westwardly by land of John Hulme and eastwardly by land by William Turner.

The plot measures in length twenty eight yards or thereabouts and breadth fourteen yards and is part of an allotment of land containing One acre, three roods and thirty one perches allotted.

Sold with all ways, waters, watercourses, hedges, ditches, mounds, fences. profits, privileges advantages and appurtenances.

Conditions/promises of land use
To permit a Chapel or Meeting house to be erected as a place of public worship by Protestant dissenters from the established Church of Congregational persuasion commonly called Independents.

So the deed was done and land purchased, and eventually a Chapel was built. The Chapel we understand was of a simple structure being built of tin.

Tomkin Chapel - 1837-8
The minutes of the Tabernacle Independent Chapel for the 6th August 1837 states the following:-

"The Pastor stated that the new Chapel at the Tomkin in the Moorlands was in a state of forwardness and that a religious service would probably be held there shortly.

It was agreed that Clement Pass who had occasionally preached in the village for some time past should at the next church meeting address the Church with a view to receiving their sanction to the continuance of these exercises".

Clement Pass by trade had been a clock and watch maker but eventually became an Independent Minister, and by 1871 was living in Oldbury, Worcestershire with members of his family.

The Congregation Association Report for 1838 reported "The inhabitants for several miles around were previously in the greatest religious destitution, but now, for nearly 12 months the chapel, which seats 100 persons, is usually well filled from the scattered population. This place is chiefly supplied by lay preachers from the surrounding churches, without any cost to the Association. But a good man, who has many years been a member of the church meeting in the Tabernacle, Hanley, has been employed by the Association in circulating religious tracts, conversing with the people, holding prayer meetings, etc. in this district, who services have been exceedingly useful in awakening attention to public worship and it is hoped to the truths of the gospel. It is intended to establish a Sabbath school among the people immediately".

This report stated that the Chapel in 1838 sat 100, it could well have done, particularly at this time, but today the Chapel sits about 50.

After 1838
Very little is known about the period between 1838 and 1860, but we know that it gets a brief mention in the **1861 Census – Tomkin Chapel Independent**

Tomkin Chapel is dated 1865. It is presumed that this is when a brick structure replaced the one of tin.

1881 Census - Tomskin Chapel

1885 – North Staffordshire Congregation and South Staffordshire Congregation amalgamated to become the "Staffordshire Congregational Union" having their first annual general meeting in this year. Annual meetings were held every year from then on in different locations in the district.

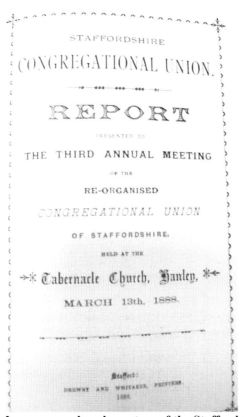

> **Congregational Union
> Annual Report
> 13 March 1888**

Image reproduced courtesy of the Staffordshire Record Office D5547/1/11

CHURCHES

forming the Staffordshire Congregational Union.

Population of the whole County in 1881, 981,385; Churches, 51; Branch
Churches, 18; Mission Stations, 12; Church Members (estimated number) 4,500
Sittings provided in Churches and Mission Stations, about 30,000.

I.—NORTHERN DISTRICT.

Treasurer—Mr. W. H. PLATT, Manchester and District Bank, Longton.
Secretary—Mr. T. W. HARRISON, Northwood, Hanley.

Church, or Branch Church, or Mission Station.	Organized.	Pastor or Evangelist.	Settled.
ASHLEY	1841	Lay Agency	
BURSLEM—	1821	T. Hartley	1882
Queen Street			
Wycliffe Hall	1885		
CHEADLE	1800	J. W. H. Snell	1877
DRESDEN	1868	J. H. Howshall	1876
HALMEREND	1819	Lay Agency	
NEWCASTLE-UNDER-LYME	1781	W. J. Websdale	1886
HANLEY—			
The Tabernacle	1784	T. K. Higgs, M.A.	1878
Mission Hall	1879	and Lay Agency	
Hope Chapel	1812	W. Landsell, B.A.	1886
Tomkin	1837	Lay Agency	
*Welsh Church	1850	Lay Agency	
LEEK—			
Derby Street	1695	J. Hankinson	1856
Allsop St. Mission	1876	G. J. Cole	1886
Ball Hay Green	1882	and Lay Agency	
Angle Street	1887		
LONGTON	1818	J. Willcox	1886
MILTON	1828	J. H. Partridge	1886
SILVERDALE	1872	and Lay Agency	
*OAKAMOOR	1864	C. Denman	1874
STAFFORD—	1786	S. B. Handley	1865
Great Haywood	1846	and Lay Agency	
STOKE-ON-TRENT	1849	W. Pearson	1886
STONE	1786	W. Nicholson	1875
Eccleshall	1824	Lay Agency	
TEAN	1808	Lay Agency	
TUNSTALL	1853	E. Constant	1885
TUTBURY	1799	J. Wolfendale	1859
UTTOXETER	1792	R. Barker	1853

* Not in the Union.

Image reproduced courtesy of the Staffordshire Record Office D5547/1/11

Tomkin does not feature very often in the Annual reports. It was recorded annually that the Deeds to the Chapel were deposited in the Union Deed box, which were in the possession of the Treasurer.

Most Churches submitted annual financial statements, revealing collections, subscriptions and contributions etc. Tomkin never did which leaves us a little in the dark regarding income and expenditure.

Collections and Subscriptions 1887

North Staffordshire.

Previous Year. £ s. d.		Collections. £ s. d.	Subscriptions. £ s. d.	Totals. £ s. d.
1 1 0	Abbots Bromley	2 2 0		2 2 0
0 10 6	Ashley		0 10 6	0 10 6
Nil	Burslem	2 2 0		2 2 0
Nil	Cheadle	0 10 0		0 10 0
1 16 0	Team	1 10 0		1 10 0
Nil	Halmerend			Nil
Nil	Silverdale	2 2 0		2 2 0
12 0 0	Hanley Tabernacle	12 0 0		12 0 0
24 18 0	Leek	5 0 0		5 0 0
1 1 0	Longton, Caroline Street	1 1 0		1 1 0
4 15 0	Do. Belgrave Road	1 10 0	1 10 0	3 0 0
11 3 0	Newcastle	4 0 0	7 14 0	11 14 0
6 18 6	Stafford	1 1 0	3 0 0	4 1 0
3 3 6	Stoke-on-Trent			Nil
14 10 9	Stone	4 15 2	4 11 0	9 6 2
Nil	Tomkin			Nil
3 12 0	Tunstall	4 2 0	3 5 6	7 7 6
1 0 0	Tutbury	1 0 0		1 0 0
6 3 7	Uttoxeter	1 17 5	3 19 6	5 16 11
2 17 7	Wolstanton		5 10 6	5 10 6
3 19 6	Chesterton	1 1 0	3 8 6	4 9 6
2 17 11	Autumnal Meeting	2 15 4		2 15 4
£103 8 10		£48 8 11	33 9 6	81 18 5

Image reproduced courtesy of the Staffordshire Record Office D5547/1/11

Annual Union Financial Reports (1885-1974) revealed that Tomkin never asked for a grant or any financial assistance.

The only other brief mention in the annual reports was for the year 1893-4. The Chairman wrote:-

"Passing to the smaller Churches, there are some that we must bear in mind though they ask for no money, places like Eccleshall, Ashley, Milton, and Tomkin in the North, places like Gentleshaw, Langley Green, Rushell in the South; and we must remember that though we begin the year with a surplus (financial), that surplus will be required from the Committee if we have to deal at an early date with Armitage, Cannock and Hednesford, Well Street and Shelton".

Confirming that Tomkin had been self sufficient throughout its earlier history.

SEPTEMBER 27, 1902.

S. Sentinel

CONGREGATIONAL WORK IN NORTH STAFFORDSHIRE.

A REVIEW OF THE COUNTY UNION.

The interesting review which follows of the work of the North Staffordshire Congregational Union, particularly since 1851, was given by Mr. G. W. Garlick at the autumnal meeting of the Northern Division of the County Union at Longton last week:—The North Staffordshire Congregational Union was established at Stone in 1793, and re-organised at Leek in 1851. It was united with the South Staffordshire Union in April, 1885. It appears, however, from the speech of Alderman Cooksey at Wolverhampton in 1885 that a Congregational Union for the whole of Staffordshire was formed in that town in the year 1814, and that it continued until 1850, but in 1851 the Churches of the northern part formed a separate union. It appears from the statement that the northern part of the county had a separate union of the Congregational Churches for twenty-one years, from 1793 to 1814, then a period of 36 years of union with the south, then a further period of 35 years as a separate union. Again it had a further period of 17 years in union with the south—so that its total existence, separate and united, is a period of 109 years.

It was not, however, until 1861 that I came to Staffordshire and became connected with your Union. I can, therefore, only speak personally of matters since that date. Unfortunately, after trying to obtain copies of the previous years' reports I have failed. It is a pity that we have no system by which our official reports and statistics can be accurately and methodically filed and preserved. The oldest annual report in my possession is that for 1861-2, but I have a copy of "the constitution and government of the North Staffordsire Congregational Union," established in Union Chapel, Leek, on 25th March, 1851, which gives a list of ten pastors and thirteen churches, comprising the Union at its commencement.

The churches were as follows:—1784, the Tabernacle Chapel, Hanley; 1781, the Marsh Chapel, Newcastle; 1812, Hope Chapel, Shelton; 1821, Queen-street Chapel, Burslem; 1818, Caroline-street Chapel, Longton; 1786, Zion Chapel, Stafford; 1695, Union Chapel, Leek; 1786, Congregational Chapel, Stone; 1800, Bethel Chapel, Cheadle; 1808, Providence Chapel, Tean; 1824, Independent Chapel, Eccleshall; Congregational Chapel, Bishop's Offley; 1849, Town Hall, Stoke.

The term used "at its commencement" must mean 1851, as only five of these chapels were in existence in 1793.

In 1861, when I joined your Union, the number of churches had been increased to 23, the additions being Alton (with Denstone as a preaching station), Ashley, Burnstead, Gnosall Halmerend, Hilderstone, Derby-street (Leek), Milton, Tomkin, and Tunstall. In 1885, when the union with the south took place, the number of churches had been further increased to 25—by the additions of Alsager, Dalehall (Burslem), Dresden, Tabernacle Mission (Hanley), Silverdale, Tutbury, and Uttoxeter; and the loss of Alton (with Denstone), Burnstead, Gnosall, Hilderstone, and Bishop's Offley—which had either been sold, rented to other bodies, or given up. The last record of one, Hilderstone, is that it was in ruins. And even the gain of two was more apparent than real, as Tutbury and Uttoxeter came to us from the south. Blakeley Lane has also been

Article courtesy of The Sentinel

There is very little documented history available on the Chapel so the next reference jumps to 1902 with an article that appears in the Staffordshire Sentinel. The article is on Congregational work in North Staffordshire written by Mr. G.W. Garlick who was asked to review their work particularly since 1851. The article is a long one with Tomkin receiving a mention in the first column.

"In 1861 when I joined your Union, the member of Churches had been increased to 23, the additions being Alton, Ashley, Burntwood, Gnosall, Halmerend, Hilderstone, Derby Street, Leek, Milton, Tomkin and Tunstall"......

The next reference appears in the:-

GEORGE BARLOW, Secretary.

CHARITY COMMISSION.

In the Matter of the following CHARITIES, in the County of STAFFORD:—

1. The Charity consisting of the Congregational Chapel, in the Ancient Township of GREAT HAYWOOD, in the Ancient Parish of COLWICH, comprised in an Indenture dated 9th January, 1845;

2. The Charity consisting of the Congregational Chapel, in TOMPKIN, in the Township of BAGNALL, in the Parish of STOKE-UPON-TRENT, comprised in an Indenture dated 1st June, 1837; and

In the Matter of THE CHARITABLE TRUSTS ACTS, 1853 to 1894.

By direction of the Board of Charity Commissioners for England and Wales, NOTICE IS HEREBY GIVEN that they propose provisionally to approve and certify, after the expiration of one Calendar month, to be computed from the first publication of this notice, a SCHEME for the future regulation of the above-mentioned Charities to be submitted to Parliament.

Printed copies of the proposed Scheme may be inspected free of cost on each weekday during a period of fifteen days from the first publication of this notice, between the hours of 10 a.m. and 4 p.m. at the house of Mr. Beardmore, Little Haywood, near Stafford, and at the house of Mrs. J. Kirkham, Bagnall Grange, Bagnall, Stoke-upon-Trent, and between the hours of 10 a.m. and 4 p.m. at the Office of the Commissioners, where also copies may be purchased during the same period at the price of 3d. each, which may be remitted by Postal Order, crossed "Bank of England," or, if the amount be less than One Shilling, in penny postage stamps.

Any objections to the proposed Scheme or suggestions thereon must be transmitted to the said Commissioners in writing within one month next after the first publication of this notice, addressed to "The Secretary, Charity Commission ..."

Dated this 5th day of October, 1911.

HENRY W. T. BOWMAN, Secretary.

Article courtesy of The Sentinel

Published notification from the Charity Commission regarding Tomkin Congregational Chapel, published in the Staffordshire Sentinel, regarding the Charities Trusts Acts 1853-1894. The above acts were extended to Tomkin and sealed by order of the Board of the Charity Commission on the 29th September 1911. No objections were received and the proposal was approved and the meeting of 25th March 1912 "subject to confirmation by Act of Parliament".

County Union and Home Churches Fund

Between 1958 and 1971 it was recorded that Tomkin made a number of payments/donations to the County Union & Home Churches Fund

The fund went to Ministers, Retired Ministers, Ministers Widows, Lay Preachers and to the Churches.

They made the following donations/payments:-

1958-1962   £1 per annum
1963-1965   £5 per annum

In 1966 it then changed to the County Union and Home and Overseas Fund no payments were made for a few years.

1968-1971 they made donations of £5 per annum to the Mission Fund and £5 per annum to the Home Fund.

In **1978** the Church was amalgamated they became known at the United Reformed Church.

From the 1980's the Chapel has had its up and downs.

In **1984** the Chapel almost closed due to it needing major repairs; £2000 was needed for essential maintenance. Mrs Helen Bailey, Mrs Jean McNicol and Mrs Cynthia Brammer formed an action group to raise money for the work, along with a grant and some help from voluntary workers of the Manpower Services Commission the three were successful in their mission, and the Chapel was refurbished.

Services were held at Mission in Stanley while the work was being done.

The Chapel had a new roof, a new floor, walls were fitted with wood panelling, the tiny kitchen was refurbished and they also purchased a new electric organ to replace the one that was stolen.

All the work undertaken was in-keeping with the building and they were fortunate enough to obtain a pulpit from Great Haywood Chapel, an alter rail from Kingsley Holt Chapel and the wood to make a wooden cross and notice board came from Maybank Methodist Chapel.

Photograph courtesy of Leek Post and Times – 3 Jan 1985

Tomkin Chapel during restoration

Leek Post and Times - May 1985
Tomkin was saved, after having major repairs undertaken it was ready to commence Sunday services once again.

Photograph courtesy of Leek Post and Times May 1985
Jean McNicol, Helen Bailey and Cynthia Brammer, Tomkin Chapel

June 16th 1985

The Chapel reopened again, with Reverend Eric Carless – conducting the rededication service. The following photographs were all taken on this special occasion.

Cynthia Brammer, a representative from the Manpower Services, Pam Beech, Reverend Eric Carless, Derek Harris, Jean McNicol, Helen Bailey, and Harold Baggaley (from Longton Church).

Mary Allsopp, Brenda McNicol and Gillian Bailey

Eric Docksey, Organist

Janet Pearson, Derek Harris, Harold Baggaley and Margaret Harris

Cyril Moss, Edith Steele(back) Ada Salmon, Joan & Rosemary Steele, ? in stripped hat, Mrs Boyyer in chequered coat, Mrs Kelsall in between Albert and Arthur Docksey and Harold Bagguley under Chapel window

Only five regular worshippers left, but . . .

Women keep their tiny chapel open

Mrs. Helen Bailey, left, Mrs. Jean McNichol and Mrs. Cynthia Brammer, right, at the tiny United Reform Chapel at Tompkin, near Stanley.

Photograph courtesy of The Sentinel

1985- Although the Chapel had been refurbished services were now held once a month instead of weekly due to low attendance.

1990 – Received Certificate of the registry of a building for the solemnisation of marriages – 13th October 1990.

SUPERINTENDENT REGISTRAR'S CERTIFICATE OF THE REGISTRY OF A BUILDING
FOR THE SOLEMNISATION OF MARRIAGES THEREIN

I hereby Certify *that a Building named*

UNITED REFORMED CHURCH

situated at TOMKIN, BAGNALL

in the Registration District of STAFFORDSHIRE MOORLANDS

in the Non-Metropolitan County / ~~Metropolitan District / London Borough~~ of STAFFORDSHIRE

being a Building certified according to law as a place of meeting for Religious Worship, was on the THIRTIETH day of OCTOBER 1990 duly registered for solemnizing Marriages therein, pursuant to Section 41 of the Marriage Act, 1949, as amended by Section 1 (1) of the Marriage Acts Amendment Act, 1958.

Witness my hand this TWELFTH day of NOVEMBER 1990.

J. M. Taylor
Superintendent Registrar

1991 – First marriage took place

1996 – October. The Chapel closed for what they believed was the last time. The Chapel was also under threat of being sold.

1997- December. Chapel opened again – After discussions with representatives from the United Reformed Church it was decided to reopen the chapel as a "Mission Project". This meant that it would run for 12 months on a trial basis and the administration would be done elsewhere. First service held before Christmas and was extremely successful with a full attendance.

1998 – February. Meetings now held fortnightly.

1998 – April. Reverend Kevin Jones based at Longton was the Minister in charge at this time. He had support from two elders from local churches to give advice, Maurice Williams from Wolstanton, and John Davey from Uttoxeter.

Tomkin Chapel resurrected

by Charles Malkin

AS CHRISTIANS prepare to mark the resurrection of Jesus this Easter, worshippers at a little known church are to celebrate their own tiny miracle.

Back in October 1996, Tomkin Chapel, on the road from Stanley to Cheddleton, held what was believed to be its final service.

The chapel was closed and plans were made to sell the building.

Although this seemed to be the end, a small group of people in the community decided to see if the chapel could be reopened.

After many meetings and discussions with representatives from the United Reformed Church, it was decided to reopen the chapel as a Mission Project. In other words, it will run initially for 12 months, with various administrative functions performed elsewhere.

But if the church is still flourishing at the end of this time, it will become a fully fledged chapel in its own right.

VIABLE

The first service was held on the Sunday before last Christmas to see if there was enough support in the area to make the chapel viable.

The small building was almost filled with people so more services were planned for this year, beginning in February on a fortnightly basis.

So far, average attendance has been between 12 and 20 worshippers of all ages, and it is hoped numbers will continue to grow.

To celebrate this "resurrection," the chapel will be open over the Easter weekend of April 11 and 12, from 10am to 4pm, with displays of flowers and items relating to local history and the life of the community as well as with artefacts from the chapel's past.

Said the Rev Kevin Jones, minister in charge: "Through people's faith in God and their commitment to keep on trying, Tomkin Chapel has come back to life."

Article courtesy of Leek Post and Times April 1st 1998

Celebration for chapel that rose from dead

BY MARIA SCRIVENS

AS CHRISTIANS the world over celebrate Easter and the rise of Christ from the dead, a remote chapel is celebrating a resurrection of its own.

The Tomkin Chapel in the Staffordshire Moorlands held what was believed to be its final service in October 1996 since only four people were attending monthly services.

However, plans to sell off the chapel were halted when a group of people contacted the Rev Kevin Jones of Longton United Reformed Church to see if it could be reopened.

After meetings with URC representatives, it was decided to open the chapel as a Mission Project and the first service was on the Sunday before Christmas when it was filled to the rafters.

Since February, services have been fortnightly and to celebrate its resurrection, the chapel hold an open weekend on Saturday and Sunday.

Minister for the Mission, Mr Jones said: "Churches have been supportive about getting it started. The Uttoxeter URC has given a communion table and we've had donations of hymn books."

"The services have taken place on Sunday afternoon to try to fit in with farming hours and we've been averaging about 16 people, although the most was 22 which is more than half full."

Tomkin Chapel will be open over the weekend from 10am - 4pm with floral displays, items relating to the history and life of the community along with artifacts from the chapels past.

These include the wedding dress of a bride who was married at the chapel and Sunday school prizes.

The congregational chapel is believed to date back to 1860's although there are gravestones which pre-date the building. The land is believed to have been donated by a local farmer.

Worship is being shared with Rev Barry Griffith and Rev Ivor Davies, although the Rev Kevin Jones will be leading the celebration service on Easter Sunday at 2.30pm.

Mr Jones added: "People are enthusiastic and we are looking at a supper and music for Pentecost and a strawberry tea in July."

"At Easter we thank God for the resurrection of Jesus and it is appropriate to celebrate, with God's love, what seemed impossible has come true. Through people's faith and commitment to keep on trying, Tomkin Chapel has come back to life."

Refreshments are being served throughout the weekend and everyone is invited.

Article courtesy of The Sentinel April 9th 1998

1998- April. Easter - Open-Weekend.
Chapel open 10-4pm with floral displays, items relating to the history and life of the community along with artefacts from the Chapels past.

Article and Photograph courtesy of Leek Post and Times -22 April 1998

Chapel comes back to life

BELOW; BLUSHING BRIDE: Jenny Phillips who was the last bride to walk down the aisle of Tomkin Chapel.

A CHAPEL which was closed in 1996 and put up for sale – has been brought back to life!

Tomkin Chapel along the Stanley to Cheddleton Road was due to close because of the lack of worshippers.

But last weekend people power was in full force, when the Chapel was formally reopened.

The Chapel was open during Easter weekend and held displays of artifacts from the Chapel's past as well as floral displays and a local history exhibition.

Also on display was the wedding dress worn by Jenny Phillips, who was the only person to be married at the church back in 1991.

1999- March 7th. A special service was held in celebration of St. David's Life and Work. This was the second occasion in the history of Tomkin that such an event took place. The Minister who officiated was the Reverend Ivor Davies who originates from the valley of South Wales. Reverend Kevin Jones, who is part Welsh, part English was present to welcome everyone to the event. Like last year visitors and members were asked to wear daffodils or leeks. Instead of tea and biscuits, tea and welsh cakes were served.

1999 – July 4th. Reverend Kevin Jones conducted his final service at Tomkin Chapel on Sunday afternoon, prior to leaving the district. Reverend Jones was instrumental in helping save the chapel by setting up a Mission there.

The Mission was given 12 months to prove itself and in that time the number of worshippers grew from a handful to around 18. The Chapel was full on special occasions; Harvest, Easter and Christmas. There have also been a number of other well supported events.

At the leaving service there were representatives from the Staffordshire District of the United Reformed Church and Mr Simon Rowntree, the Synod Clerk of the West Midlands Province of the URC who presented members of the Mission Project with certificates.

1999 – Entry from the United Reformed Church Synod Report 1999
"The Mission Project at Tomkin in North Staffordshire was reviewed during the year and Synod was pleased to note progress with growing support for this small isolated chapel".

Members - 4th July 1999

The following were made members during a special service and received a certificate of membership. Service conducted by the Reverend Jones.

Backrow from left to right
Cynthia Brammer, Emma Machin, John Bowyer, Betty Bowyer, Barbara Machin
Robert Hughes, Joan Willshaw, Joan Steele, John Royle, Reverend and Mrs Kevin Jones
Front row from left to right
Joan Kemp, Edith Steele, Fred Willshaw, Fay Butler, Michelle Hughes, Jenny Phillips with son Stephen, Mark Simcock, Ivy Simcock, Anita and Peter Rogers

Certificate of Membership presented to Joan Willshaw

(Rosemary Reade and Blanche White became members at a later date).

2000 - Entry from the United Reformed Church Synod Report 2000
"The local community continues to show great loyalty to Tomkin Chapel on the North Staffordshire Moorlands, which is still under the oversight of local ministers. On the Sunday before the last Assembly, the Chapel celebrated the willingness of over 20 adults and young people to commit themselves to its life".

2000 – June. Another open-weekend is held at the Chapel

● Villagers have joined forces to save the Tompkin Chapel from closure. Seen here at the chapel is project organiser Cynthia Brammer (right) with members of the community.
Photo: NEIL HULSE

Photograph and following article courtesy of the Sentinel – 9th June 2000

The Sentinel reported:-

"For years it was the centre of village life, a place of worship and a meeting point for families. But over the years the number of worshippers dropped and the little chapel at Tomkin was doomed to close. The small stone building was almost sold – but saved by a band of determined villagers.

Now almost two years later, the chapel is again the centre of village life, a thriving community centre and a tribute to team working and neighbourly spirit.

To celebrate its new lease of life, the chapel will be open to the public all weekend, housing exhibitions and demonstrations of local craft work, as well as cake stalls and cream tea sessions.

Cynthia Brammer, aged 50, was one of the saviours of Tomkin's little chapel. She said "Numbers attending the services were dropping, so the United Reformed Church were left with no option but to close it down. When the villagers heard about it they all decided this was not going to happen and fought to keep the chapel open. People worked on the building and organised community events which could be staged in between the fortnightly services. Now it is thriving and we hold classes, harvest suppers as well as church services. In fact we had a christening in there last weekend- the second this year. Today you hear about the doom and gloom of places closing down and being sold, but this is a success story and we are going from strength to strength. This is a small community working together, and look what we have achieved".

The Chapel was built in 1865 and originally run by the old congregational church. With just six pews laid out in rows either side of the chapel building, the room is small, but can house a crowd of up to 50. Still not modernised the chapel building has no running water, something the villagers are determined to put right. Cynthia added "at the moment they had to run up and down the lane with a bucket, but we are all working hard and have applied for lottery funding, so hopefully we will soon have running water on site".

2001 – December. Members of Tomkin Chapel go Carol Singing around the village of Stanley to raise money for the Donna Louise Trust and Pat Wood's Home for stray cats and dogs. Last year the group of 30 singers managed to raise around £200, and it was hoped to do better. Cynthia Brammer was the organiser, told local papers that "we have a wonderful evening of singing which was rounded off with a Christmas meal at the pub in Stanley. We call at most homes in the village and will sing around 30 carols".

Little chapel keeps pulling them back

THERE is a hamlet in the Moorlands which is a shining example of how faith can prosper in the most isolated of communities. Tomkin is little more than a couple of cottages, a telephone box and a tiny chapel overlooking rolling countryside.

Locals are fiercely proud of this living piece of history at the heart of their community. Five years ago a dwindling congregation of just four people attending monthly services meant the building was threatened with closure. But since it reopened in February 1997, as a United Reformed Mission Project, services are now held fortnightly on the first and third Sunday of the month and attract as many as 18 people.

With only six small pews on each side it means the chapel is almost half full.

The original congregational chapel dates back to 1865 although there are gravestones which pre-date the current building. A tin hut chapel is believed to have stood on the site since 1837. Chapel secretary Cynthia Brammer said residents worked hard to keep the building alive.

She said: "The chapel really didn't want to die. Everyone pitches in and things somehow come together. We make the most of everyone's talents.

"Our tiny wooden font was stolen so we made something that would have no value to anyone else.

"We got a little white bowl and jug and the villagers made it unique to us. Jeff Harvey put transfers of a pen-and-ink sketch of the chapel on to them, and Mary Allsop, a retired gilder from Royal Doulton, gilded the rims and the handle. Before that we had to borrow a font for christenings."

The chapel has seen many christenings over the years but only two weddings. In 1991 the first bride Jennifer Rogers collected signatures from around the parish to get it solemnised for weddings and nine years later her sister Michelle also married there.

And this August Elizabeth Rogers will be the third sister to walk down the aisle in the chapel.

Their mother Anita said: "My husband Peter and I are very happy they've all been able to use the church and I hope more people will choose to get married here.

"I'm looking forward to Elizabeth's wedding and I hope it will go as well as the other two did. I hope it will be a nice day — weddings here are lovely."

The chapel serves as a meeting place for the surrounding community and often doubles as a village hall for well-attended events. Each October, to celebrate the harvest, all the pews are pushed against the walls and long trestle tables brought in.

Huge meat and potato pies are set at the ends of the tables and dished out with vegetables, school dinner style, usually with enough for everyone in the packed chapel to have second and third helpings.

The meal is followed by an auction where harvest produce is sold off to the highest bidder to raise funds. Services take place at 2.30pm, reflecting the area's farming history and, says Mrs Brammer: "It allows people to do their chores and have their dinner before the service, then get home for tea before it gets dark."

At the end of the service they put the kettle on — although there is no running water and it has be brought from a neighbouring house — and hand round biscuits, enjoying the social aspect of worship as well as the service itself.

And it is the strong friendships that have grown with the chapel that keep it so alive. A wide range of ages come together to worship and socialise, and pull together to support the chapel.

Mrs Brammer said: "Everything has been done through fund raising — the burglar alarms, new windows and restoring the altar chairs.

"We haven't had to ask for any financial help.

"This little chapel always pulls people back, it's part of their roots."

Article courtesy of The Sentinel

2002 – Planning application submitted for extension/kitchen/meeting room/toilet facilities.

2002 – Reverend Tom Carmichael left

2003– Trees at front of Chapel felled due to the roots spreading under the structure, and also in readiness for the extension/improvements.

Chapter Ten

Lay Preachers

Archibald Landon

Archie Landon was born in Newcastle on 14th January 1881. When he left
school he wished to go into the Ministry, he passed
Responsions for Oxford but was rejected because he
was the son of a working man.

By trade he was a copperplate engraver and also taught
lettering and heraldry, during his lifetime he still
managed to fulfil his calling to the Church in so many
ways.

At the age of 17 he became a lay preacher and was
actively engaged as one for over 60 years, often taking
more than a hundred services (Sunday and weeknight)
in a year, some of them at Tomkin. He was a member
of the Staffordshire Congregational Union Executive, and became its Chairman
in 1946. He was a Deacon at the Hanley Tabernacle Church and also a
prominent member of the North Staffordshire Lay Preachers Association.

Laurie Landon (Lawrence), Archibald's younger brother, was also a Lay
Preacher and took services at Tomkin.

William James Marson

William James Marson was the son Edmund and Annie Marson, and nephew to
William B Marson, Tomkin Secretary between 1932-1950.

Born in 1903 at "The Sycamores Farm" in Weston Coyney, he married Edna in
1930. He farmed at Accrington and later at Pear Tree Farm, Ball Green for 24
years before retiring to Leek circa 1964. He had 3 daughters. He died January
15th 1985.

William was a Lay Preacher. He is known to have had connections with
Tomkin Chapel preaching there occasionally. He was an active member of the
Methodist Church having received a certificate of recognition for completing 60
years service as a local preacher.

He and his wife Edna are buried with his Uncle William Blurton Marson in
Leek Cemetery.

STAFFORDSHIRE CONGREGATIONAL UNION.
Northern Division Lay Preachers' Association Plan, 1931.

President—Mr. G. BADDELEY.

Secretary—Mr. W. HUNTER, 32, Harding Road, Hanley.   *Asst. Secretary*—Mrs. A. LANDON, B.A.

Financial Secretary—Mr. A. Landon, 19, Brunswick Place, Hanley.   *Auditor*—Mr. Baddeley.

Executive Committee—Rev. E. L. Rowlands, B.A., B.D., Rev. A. Rhodes, Messrs. G. Baddeley. F. Cade,
C. Hobson, A. Landon and W. Hunter.

Plan Committee—Messrs. C. Hobson, A. Landon. F. Cade. W. Hunter. Mrs. Landon.

PREACHING STATIONS AND CHURCH SECRETARIES	Service Hours	OCTOBER				NOVEMBER					DECEMBER			
		4	11	18	25	1	8	15	22	29	6	13	20	27
ABBOTS BROMLEY Mr. R. Hollins. High St., A. B	2-30 & 6-30	×	12	×	5	×	6	×	15	×	42	×	22	×
ASHLEY —Mr. T. Morrey, Hungersheath. Mt. Drayton	11 & 2-45	9 9	45 25	27 27	11 11	41 41	15 30	⊠	25 25	6 6	14 14	13 23	19 17	10 10
CHESTERTON —Mr. H. Brittain 6, Victoria-st., Chesterton.	6	7	P	×	P	19	P	8	P	×	×	P	5	P
CHEADLE —Rev. A. A. Thomson Oakamoor.	10.45 6	25 25	× 17	× 19	28 28	25 25	25 25	× AVM	25 25	× 5	25 25	25 25	× 11	28 28
HALMEREND —Mr. D. Harrison 35; High St., Halmer End	2-30 & 6	×	×	×	×	×	×	×	×	×	×	×	×	×
LEEK, Alsop Street Mission — Mr Pedley, Cawdry Buildings.	6	19	×	19	9	14	×	1	11	22	×	5	×	×
SILVERDALE —Mr A. B. Morrall 110. Church St., Silverdale.	6	23	18	3	7	12	5	21	23	16	41	6	35	⊠
TABERNACLE MISSION, Union St., Hanley —Mr. W. Johnson, 7 Whitehouse Rd., Abbey Hulton.	6-15	5	24	21	6	23	9	7	14	⊠	44	18	11	1
TEAN —Mr. J. W. Robinson, The Coplows, Tean.	6	14	×	23	35	5	18	44	3	19	12	4	9	21
TOMKIN —Mr. W. Perkins, Tomkin, Nr. Stanley	6-30	38	19	46	AVM	39	14	4	33	26	3	23	6	42

P—Pastor.

PREACHERS :

Honorary Member :
Mr A. V. Mayland, 37 Hanley Rd., Sneyd Green

1 Mr G. Baddeley, 17 Rushton Road, Burslem
2 Mr A. H. Gibson, J.P., "Claremont" Park Lane, Congleton.
3 Mr A. Landon, 19 Brunswick Place, Hanley
4 Mr W. Hunter, 32, Harding Road, Hanley.
5 Mr F. Cade, 6 Berkley Street, Stone
6 Mr R. Conquer, 236, Cauldon Road, Hanley
7 Mr H. Brittain, 6, Victoria Street, Chesterton.
8 Mr J. P. Lawley, White-house Rd., Wolstanton
9 Mr A. L. Downes, 5, Kingsway West, Newcastle
10 Mr A. E. Martin, Bradwell Lane, Wolstanton.
11 Mr A. B. Morrall, 110, Church Street, Silverdale
12 Mr J. C. Gilbert, 8 Oak Terrace, Leek
13 Mr. Chas. Hobson, 265 High Lane, Burslem
14 Mr. S. G. Bramhall, 170, Cauldon Road, Shelton.
15 Mr. J. W. Robinson, The Coplows, Tean.
16 Mrs. C. Hobson, 265, High Lane, Burslem
17 Mrs. A. Landon, B.A., 19 Brunswick Place, Hanley
18 Mr. L. A. Landon, 92, Blurton Road, Fenton
19 Mr. W. Hudson, 17, The Villas, Stoke.
20 Mr. R. Underwood, Kingsley, Dimsdale View, Wolstanton, S-on-T.
21 Mr. H. Baggaley, 32 Gower Street, Longton.
22 Mr. S. Goodwin, 23, Birches Street, Cheadle.

23 Mr G. W. Pedley, Cawdry Buildings. Leek
24 Mr Joseph Jones, 25 North Street, Newcastle
25 Mr Reginald Morrall, 11 Abbey Street, Silverdale
26 Mrs Gilbert, 8 Oak Terrace, Leek

SPECIAL HELPERS :

27 Mr C. H. Tams, 37, Pyenest St. Shelton
28 Mr. H. Arnold, Fairlawn, Stallington-lane. Blythe
29 Mr. T. Hartley, "Wood Villa" Basford   [Bridge
30 Mr. H. Thompson, Stanley.
31 Mr. T. Henshaw, M.A., Dimmins Dale, Stockton Brook.
32 Mr. Geo. Jackson, Abbots Bromley
33 Mr. T. P. Ledgar, Claremont, Endon, S-o-T.
34 Mr. Thacker, 42, Osborne Road, Hartshill.
35 Mr. E. Hobson, 1 South Walk, Meir.
36 Mr. J. Adshead, 104, Newport Lane, Burslem.
37 Rev. Robert Hughes, Uttoxeter.
38 Mr. E. Wood.
39 Mr. H. Wright.
40 Mr. R. Hollins.
41 Miss May Ellis, 18 Beresford St., Shelton.
42 E. Moult, High Street, Tean.
43 Mr. Palmer.
44 Mr. Cotton.
45 Mr Harvey.
46 Mr W. J. Marson.

Every Preacher is expected to fulfil his own appointment or HIMSELF to get a suitable supply.

All communications concerning next plan must reach Mrs. Landon, *Assistant Sec.*, not later than Friday, Dec. 11th. *This is most important.*

Quarterly Meeting at the Tabernacle Mission, on 5th Dec. Tea at 5 o'clock. Please invite your friends to the Meeting at 6-30 to hear the Rev. W. W. Cotton on "The Preacher and his Tools."

H. Brittain, Printer, Chesterton—'Phone 66044.

Other Lay Preachers

James Bailey and his wife Helen remember with great affection many Lay Preachers who served the Chapel over many years, they include:-

Mr William Wise
Mr Joseph Jones
Mr Harry Jones
Mr Harold Baggaley
The Landon family
Mr Geoff Hurst
Miss Birkin
Mr Doug. Leake
Mr Colin Mort
Mrs Jean Avis
Mr Peter Roberts
Mr Derek and Mrs Margaret Harris
Mr Clive and Mrs Janet Parsons
Mr Vic Trinder
Miss Pam Beech
Mr David Hood

Many Lay Preachers brought family members with them and they joined in with the service.

The people who ran the Chapel along with these Lay Preachers kept Tomkin Chapel open through many difficult years, as well as having to earn their living.

Chapter Eleven

Chapel Secretaries 1905-1972

Peter Handley – Secretary 1905-1914

Peter Handley was born circa 1850 at Baddeley Green in the parish of Norton in the Moors. He married Annie Ede circa 1877. The family moved from Baddeley Green to Whiston Shaw Farm around 1889/90, where he farmed for a number of years. They had 9 children.

Peter was Secretary at Tomkin Chapel between 1905 and 1914. It is know that Albert his son attended Tomkin Sunday School in 1909 from Sunday school prizes, no doubt all the family would have attended.

The Handley Family from Whiston Shaw Farm, Cheddleton – photograph taken before 1917.
Back row, left to right, Annie, Frederick, Arthur, Hannah, Joseph, Albert, Florence,
Front row, left to right Laura, Peter Handley and Annie his wife, and James

S Handley – Secretary 1915-1925

The Congregational Yearbooks report that S Handley, from Whiston Shaw, Cheddleton, was Secretary during 1915-1925. Very little is known about S. Handley. It is believed that this may be Sarah Handley wife of Joseph who was known to be living at Tomkin Farm in 1918/19, but never actually lived at Whiston Shaw.

William Perkin – Secretary 1926-1931

William Perkin has already been covered in greater detail earlier in the book.

From left to right Annie Willshaw, May Glover (nee Perkins), William and Mabel Perkins, Ada Willshaw, unknown lady at very front. Photograph taken at The Smithy, Tomkin.

William Blurton Marson-Secretary 1932-1950

William Marson was born in 1870, named after his Grandfather, was the fourth child of Josiah and Margaret Marson (nee Blurton), from a large family, his brothers and sisters being Hester, Annie, Louisa, Howard, Margaret, Edmund, Adelaide and Harold.

It is know that his father farmed at Malt House Farm, in Cellarhead, between 1871 and 1891. Malt House Farm was at this time a 70 acre farm. In 1900 William married Mary Redfern; and by 1901 had taken over the farm. Little is know about the next 20 years. He farmed until his retirement in 1922, when he took over a smallholding, namely Heath House, Cheddleton and lived there until 1950 when William and Mary went to live with her sister at Sytch Villa, Bradnop.

William Marson served the Church all his life. He was a keen and gifted musician, for 41 years from the age of 12 he was organist at Cellarhead, serving the church and also steward and trustee for a number of years.

For about 4 years he was organist at Hulme Church, Nr Weston Coyney, and then went to Tomkin Chapel where he was Secretary for 25 years as well as organist. When they left the people of Tomkin Chapel presented them with a bible and a painting of the church in appreciation of their work.

William died on January 25th 1951 aged 82 years, and the funeral was at Leek Congregational Church, officiated by the Reverend M. S Leah (Minister) and the Reverend N Wilson (Minister of Leek Bethesda Methodist Church). A memorial service was held at Tomkin. Mary died April 29th 1974 aged 95 years they are buried at Leek Cemetery.

The Leek Post and Times reported that the death of Mr Marson "was a great loss to North Staffs Methodism".

William Marson is one of the people many locals remember today.

Congregational Year Book 1935

W. B Marson, Heath House, Cheddleton

CHURCHES FORMING THE STAFFORDSHIRE CONGREGATIONAL UNION.
NORTHERN DISTRICT.

Secretary—Rev. A. RHODES, St. George's Avenue, Wolstanton, Stoke-on-Trent.
Treasurer—Mr. ARTHUR JOHNSON, 104, Princes Road, Hartshill, Stoke-on-Trent.

Church, date of formation and number of sittings			Minister or Lay Pastor, and date of Settlement		Church Members	Scholars on Books	Teachers	Lay Preachers	Secretary's Name and Address
ABBOTS BROMLEY ...	1830	100	Lay Agency ...	—	—	12	38	3	—	H. Lakin, 143 Leek Road, Smallthorne, S.O.T.
BURSLEM ...	1821	550	Vacant ...	—	—	267	152	33	4	Rev. A. A. M. Thomson, Oakamoor (pro. tem.)
CHEADLE ...	1797	350	J. Iorwerth Price	1931	25	40	4	1	J. W. Robinson, The Coplows, Tean.
TEAN ...	1808	180			55	46	4	1	
HALMEREND ...	1834	150	Lay Agency ...	—	—	28	108	12	2	O. Harrison, 35, High Street, Halmerend.
SILVERDALE ...	1873	480	Vacant ...	—	—	50	110	13	1	A. B. Morrall, 110, Church Street, Silverdale.
HANLEY: Hope ...	1810	500			70	200	32	2	F. P. White, 46, Boulton Street, Hanley.
Park ...	1899	450							{ H. Pointon, Cotwalton, Park Road, Basford.
Tabernacle ...	1784	1050	Arthur Oates, M.A.	1931	215	250	31	3	{ W. H. Marshall, M.A., 108, Wellesley Street, Hanley.
Union Street ...	1879	300			79	207	18	—	A. Lancaster, 204, Bryan Street, Hanley.
*Mayer Street ...	1850	350	W. Williams ...	1900	41	8	2	—	J. Williams, 47 Hammersley Street, Birches Head,
LEEK ...	1695	600	S. W. Green, B.A., B.D.	1928	250	170	28	2	S. Stannard, J.P., The Park, Leek. [Hanley.
with Alsop St. Mission ...	1876	250	Lay Agency ...	—	—	46	8	—	G. W. Pedley, Cawdry Buildings, Leek.
LONGTON: Caroline Street ...	1818	500	Mr. A. R. Mellor	1928	102	267	23	2	W. A. Beresford, Star and Garter Road, Longton.
Belgrave Road ...	1868	450	Mr. E. Walton ...	1925	90	160	20	1	F. H. Kinsey, 22 Spring Road, Normacot.
NEWCASTLE ...	1781	500	Vacant ...	—	178	160	25	—	H. Makinson, 14 Milehouse Lane, Newcastle.
ASHLEY ...	1841	150		—	17	5	1	—	T. Morrey, "Hungersheath" Ashley, Market Drayton
STAFFORD ...	1786	600	Silvester Davies,	1930	180	95	15	2	J. F. Amery, "Lorema" Radford Bank. Stafford.
with Great Haywood ...	1886	75	M.A., B.D. ...		7	16	2	—	
STOKE ...	1849	450	H. J. G. Potter ...	1927	89	157	19	2	H. W. Pointon, 21 Grove Road, Penton.
STONE ...	1786	800	O. J. Beard, B.A.	1928	189	208	33	—	L. Welch, Townley House, Stone.
TOMKIN ...	1837	30	Lay Agency ...	—	—	12	—	—	W. B. Marson, Heath House, Cheddleton.
TUNSTALL ...	1853	500	E. T. George ...	1929	132	216	35	2	F. Clewes, 35 Davenport Street, Tunstall.
TUTBURY ...	1799	400	Vacant ...	—	60	84	10	—	F. Crossley, Corn Mill Lane, Tutbury.
UTTOXETER ...	1788	350	R. Hughes, A.T.S.	1915	91	76	10	—	W. E. Elkes, High Street, Uttoxeter.
WOLSTANTON ...	1902	450	A. Rhodes ...	1915	180	200	18	4	A. E. Martin, 41 Bradwell Lane, Porthill.
CHESTERTON ...	1894	250			62	200	13	1	H. Brittain, 6 Victoria Street, Chesterton.
*OAKAMOOR ...	1878	200	A. A. M. Thomson	1926	—	49	7	—	Wm. Coates, Sunnyside, Oakamoor.
* Church not in the Union.									

Image reproduced courtesy of the Staffordshire Record Office

Lay Preachers Annual Meeting 1939 (location of scene unknown)
6th from right standing, Doreen Wincle, 2nd left kneeling W.B. Marson

Alice Ann Riley (nee Proctor)-Secretary 1951-1975

Alice Riley was born Alice Ann Proctor in Fawfieldhead, Longnor in 1905, the daughter of George and Emma Proctor. She married James Riley at St. Luke's Church, Leek, in 1943. At the time of their marriage James Riley was already living and farming at The Smithy at Tomkin and after they married it became the family home. For a time James' parents, Joseph and Hannah Riley lived with them at The Smithy.

The Congregational Year Books indicate that Mrs Riley became Secretary at Tomkin Chapel in 1951 and held this post for 24 years. The Riley's lived here until 1965, when they moved to "Chale" in Endon village. Mrs Riley continued with her work as Treasurer and Secretary at the Chapel until her death in 1975. Mrs Riley died 30th May 1975 and was buried at St. Bartholomew's Church in Longnor.

Congregational Year Book 1961- Tomkin

The second column refers to seating places available – Tomkin sat 30
The entry for Tomkin is the same in the Year Book for 1963-64 and 1966-67

Place	Est.	Seats	Minister / Status	Year					Address
LONGTON, Caroline-st. ..	1818	500	} Vacant	..	60	45	6	1	W. Baker, 157, Brocksford-st., Fenton, Stoke-on-Trent
LONGTON, Belgrave-rd.	1868	450	}		32	52	8	2	G. Holloway, 15, Beccleugh-rd., Longton, Stoke-on-Trent [on-Trent
TEAN	1808	180	Vacant	..	67	35	4	1	J. Hurst, The Stores, High-st., Tean, Stoke-
NEWCASTLE-UNDER-LYME	1781	500	D. J. Mills, BA	1959	104	99	21	2	H. Makinson, 28, Pilkington-avenue, Newcastle-under-Lyme (Tel. 66342)
Ashley	1841	150	Lay agency..........	..	5				Mrs. Harvey, The Rock, Ashley, Market Drayton, Salop
OAKAMOOR, Free Church	1878	200	J. A. Powell........	1959	43	16	3		Miss June Bolton, Lightoaks, Oakamoor, Stoke-on-Trent, Staffs (Tel. 207)
STAFFORD	1786	600	M. W. Gandy (B) ..	1960	87	70	14	2	W. R. George, B.SC, 72, Burton Manor-rd., Stafford (Tel. 1616) [Stafford
Great Haywood	*1886*	75	Supplied	..	8	12	1		H. Eyre, Coley-lane, Little Haywood,
STONE	1786	800	J. H. Collins	1956	114	83	12		E. D. Aston, 3, Heathfield Grove, Sandon-rd., Meir, Stoke-on-Trent (Tel. Blythe Bridge 2229)
TOMKIN	1837	30	Lay agency..........	..					J. A. Riley, Tomkin Smithy, Stanley, Stoke-on-Trent (Tel. 200)
TUNSTALL	1853	500	Vacant..............	..	80	70	12	1	S. A. Cooper, 29, Jaycean-avenue, Tunstall, Stoke-on-Trent on-Trent
SILVERDALE	1873	480	} G. M. Taylor	1960	38	40	6	4	H. Brooks, 7, Park-rd., Silverdale, Stoke-
CHESTERTON	1894	250	}		71	80	12	4	S. A. Cooper, 6, Victoria-st., Chesterton, Stoke-on-Trent (Tel. 68044)
UTTOXETER	1788	350	K. W. Marvin	1938	95	60	9	1	Miss L. M. Elkes, 21, Carter-st., Uttoxeter (Tel. 517) [Stoke-on-Trent
WOLSTANTON	1902	450	R. Royston-Bishop ..	1960	180	230	20	4	A. E. Martin, 31, Bradwell-lane, Porthill,

STAFFORDSHIRE UNION

The North Staffordshire Lay Preachers' Association supplies most of the village stations.

Image reproduced courtesy of the Staffordshire Record Office

1973-1982 – Helen Bailey, Jean McNicol

1982-1996 – Helen Bailey, Jean McNicol and Cynthia Brammer

1997- 1999 - Cynthia Brammer

1999 – to present - Joan Willshaw (Treasurer), Cynthia Brammer

Chapter Twelve

Baptisms, Marriages, Burials and Memorial Services

Baptisms

We are aware that many baptisms have taken place at Tomkin, but at present cannot locate any Chapel Parish Records to support this. The Chapel had a small font which was stolen some years ago and replaced by members a few years ago.

Marriages

Harwicke's Marriage Act came into force on 25th March 1754. The purpose of the Act was to prevent clandestine marriages, where marriages had taken place without banns been read or marriage licences being obtained. This Act prevented marriages taking place in any other place than the parish church.

The marriage process has changed a great deal since those days so when in 1990 Jennifer Rogers wanted to get married in the Chapel she had to petition to get the Chapel solemnised. She collected signatures from across the parish so that the Chapel could undertake weddings, she was successful and the Chapel received permission.

Jennifer and husband Lawrence Phillips

Jennifer with her father Peter

Since that eventful date 2 more of Jennifer's sisters have married at the Chapel.

Robert Hughes and Michelle Rogers married at Tomkin on Saturday October 14th 2000. Only the second couple to stride down the aisle.

Michelle and Robert both attended Chapel regularly. Michelle's parents Peter and Anita Rogers live at Acres Barn Farm, in Tomkin Lane, Stanley they are also members of the Chapel.

Photograph courtesy of The Sentinel – 13 Oct 2000

Register of Marriages Tomkin Chapel

Jennifer Rogers married Lawrence Phillips 31 August 1991

Michelle Rogers married Robert Hughes 14 October 2000

Elizabeth Rogers married Andrew Hollins 17 August 2002

Burials

Memorials in Churchyard

It is intriguing to find that there are a number of headstones at Tomkin. It is rare for non-conformist Chapels to have burial grounds.

Memorials in any Churchyard can normally provide a wealth of information and although there are only 4 headstones in the ground of the Chapel, they can still be informative.

It is said that the graveyard is full; it is possible that there are a few more headstones present which maybe lying flat and covered by grass.

The stones here date about from about the middle to late nineteenth century, the earliest burial being 1838 and the latest 1897.

The James family

> Sacred
> To the Memory of Amy daughter of Joseph and Sarah James of Tomkin who died January 16th 1870 aged 13 years and 8 months
> Weep not she is not dead but sleepeth
>
> Also the above named Joseph James of Brunswick Place, Hanley, Late of Tomkin who departed this life April 13 1878 aged 61 years
> Grieve not dear wife for I am at rest
> Grieve not dear children for I am blest
> Grieve not dear friends for I've left a world of care
> To meet my God – To follow me prepare
>
> Also Sarah James the beloved wife of the above who departed this life July 26th 1884 aged 67 years
>
> Thy will be done

The James family moved to Tomkin after 1861, they were certainly living here at the time of their daughter Amy's death in 1870 and still here in 1871 when the Census was taken. James was a coal miner, and by 1878 the family had moved to Hanley. The 1881 Census tells that Sarah James was aged 64, a widow and her occupation is given as a Housekeeper, on the night of the Census she was living alone at 10 Brunswick Place, Stoke-on-Trent.

The Smith family

> Phoebe Wife of James Smith of Rose Bank, Cheddleton
> Who died June 13th 1870 aged 84 years
> I spent this life in strife and care
> But now I rest in hope of eternal life
>
> In loving Memory of Joseph Smith
> Son of the above who died July 23rd 1897
> Aged 82 years
>
> Thy will be done

Phoebe Foster was born circa 1789. She married James Smith (born circa 1788-1790) on the 3rd October 1811 at Leek.

In 1851 James, his wife Phoebe and their son Ralph and his wife Elizabeth, were living and farming a 50 acre farm in Park Lane, Endon.

In 1861 James, Phoebe and their son Joseph were farming at Rose Bank Farm in Cheddleton; they had a house servant named Mary Morton.

By 1871, Phoebe had died and the farm had been taken over by their son Ralph, his wife Elizabeth and 3 children, his father James, aged 83, lived with them at the farm.

Joseph, son of Phoebe and James was born c. 1815, he married widow Martha Billinge in 1868 and by 1871 were living at Acres Barn in Stanley a short distance from Rose Bank Farm, by 1891 Joseph was a widower and he and his sister Ellen were living back at Rose Bank Farm sharing the farm with his brother Ralph.

The Inscription leads us to believe that Mrs Smith had a very hard life.

The Turner family

In Memory of William Turner who died Aug 10th 1839
aged 79 years

In Memory of Ann wife of W Turner who died March 26th
1838 aged 78 years

Farewell dear children our time is past
We loved you while life did last
Weep not for us you weep in vain
Weep for your sins and then refrain

William Turner was born circa 1760, and married Ann Stanway on the 25th October 1784 at Cheddleton.

William was a Wheelwright and living at Bagnall Grange Farm in 1837, he was also a landowner, some of which he sold to the Trustees of Tomkin Chapel. William and Ann had 5 children, Enoch, William, Samuel, Dorothy and Martha. Enoch emigrated to Toronto, Canada, circa 1830-31, who after a number of setbacks eventually became very prosperous. He made a gift of a Schoolhouse to the Church (Anglican) and throughout his lifetime supported the church personally and financially. The School today is a museum.

William actually died in 1840 it appears a mistake was made on the memorial Stone, he wrote and signed his will June 20th 1840. By this time he had moved to Werrington and it was his son Samuel who was living at Bagnall Grange Farm.

In his will he requested that his books and tools be divided equally between William and Samuel if they could do so amicably.

He made a bequest to Enoch who was resident in Toronto, Canada, the sum of five pounds as a testimonial of respect.

He left the house, land and premises known as Hodgefields in Brown Edge, between William, Samuel and his daughter Dorothy (Cape). Dorothy was resident in Van Dieman's Land, (Re-named Tasmania from 1856, an island state of Australia). He made a condition that Dorothy Cape should claim her share in 12 months, or it would go jointly between his sons William and Samuel.

It is possible that Dorothy and her husband left for Australia at the same time as the Reverend Newland Ridgway, to undertake some kind of missionary work, many convicts were transported there between 1803-1852.

To his daughter Martha (Lockett) for the time of her natural life he left the weekly sum of two shillings and sixpence and also made his freehold estate at the Tomkin in the parish of Stoke on Trent in the occupation of Alexander Edge chargeable with the aforesaid weekly legacy, and at his daughter Martha Lockett's decease, her gave all the residue of the estate to William, Samuel and Dorothy Cape on the same condition as before that Dorothy should claim her share within 12 months of Martha's death. If she should fail to do so then it would go again to Samuel and William, and out of Samuel's share he should give the sum of twenty pounds to his Grandson William Turner.

The Billinge Family

> To the memory of
> Isaac Billinge
> Late of Little Eves and son of Isaac and
> Sarah Billinge of New House
> Who died June 28 1855 aged 26 years
> Also Elizabeth his second daughter aged
> 14 days
>
> Weep not dear friends it is in rain
> The time will come to meet again
> Our days earth they were but few
> And past away like morning dew.

Headstone lies flat on the ground

Isaac Billinge was born in Longnor circa 1829; he married Martha Conder in 1850 at St. Edwards Church, Leek. Isaac was an agricultural labourer. By 1851 Isaac and Martha had moved to Stanley and then to Tomkin about 1852/3. Isaac died in 1855 aged 26.

The 1861 Census described Martha Billinge as a widow and a School Mistress. She had 3 children; Sarah aged 9, Charlotte aged 7 and Elizabeth aged 3.

Martha later married Joseph Smith late of Rose Bank Farm in a civil marriage at Leek in 1868. They later moved to Acres Barn, Stanley.

Memorial Service

Memorial services will have taken place at Tomkin throughout its history, the most notable being the following:-

Albert Handley

IN LOVING MEMORY OF

ALBERT,

Beloved Son of Peter and Annie Handley,

of Whiston Shaw Farm, Cheddleton,

Who was killed in France November 11th, 1917,

By a bursting Shell,

AGED 25 YEARS.

A Memorial Service will be held in Tomkin Chapel, on Dec. 23, at 6-15, by Mr. A. V. Mayland, of Hanley.

Albert son of Peter and Annie Handley was killed during the 1st World War. Albert Handley was a Pioneer of the Royal Engineers (63rd Field Coy), and was killed in November 1917. A memorial service was held at Tomkin December 23rd.

William Marson

William and Mary Marson left Heath House, Cheddleton in 1950, and moved to live with Mary's sister at Sytch House, Bradnop. William Marson was Tomkin Chapel Secretary and Organist from 1932-1950. A Memorial Service was held on February 4th at Tomkin.

In Loving Memory of

William Blurton Marson
Beloved husband of Mary
Late of Heath House, Cheddleton
Died 25 January 1951
Aged 82 years

A Memorial Service will be held in Tomkin Chapel
on February 4th at 6.15pm

Chapter Thirteen

Sunday school - Annual Book Awards

It is not known when the Annual awards started, but evidence supports that they were undertaken as far back as 1893, and continued until 1968/9 a tradition lasting over 70 years. The following represent just a few of the many presented with books between this period of time.

My Brother's Life by R.B. Wainwright was presented to George Willshaw in 1893.

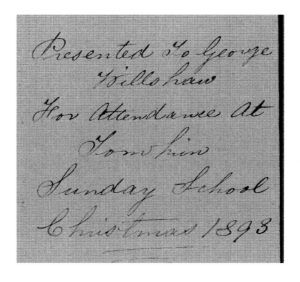

George Willshaw was born in 1885 and lived with his family at Black Bank Farm. George was known to attend Sunday school at Tomkin between 1892-1897. He lived and farmed in Cheddleton all his life.

The Holy Bible- presented to Charles Edge 1900

Book presentations probably continued, but no evidence has been found to support this. The next book award found/recorded was to Arthur Willshaw (26 years later). Arthur was born in 1916, and was known to attend Tomkin Sunday School between 1926-27. Arthur died in 1928 aged 11.

A dog with a bad name, by Talbot N Reed presented to Arthur Willshaw in 1926

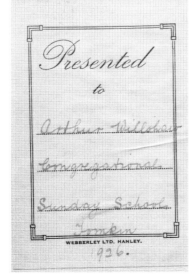

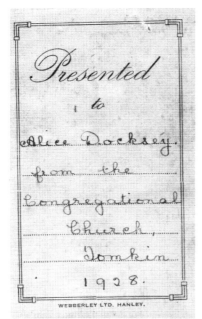

TOMKIN

Much sympathy is extended to Mr. and Mrs. Docksey and family in their sad bereavement in losing their only daughter, Alice Mary (a girl in her early teens), who was a devoted scholar in our Sunday School for a number of years. Her death took place on November 24th. Alice underwent an operation two years ago, which accounted for her completely losing her eyesight. She had been very contented and most cheerful throughout her long illness.

We are pleased that the Rev. S. Withers Green visited the dear girl many times as also did Mrs. Gilbert and her Sunday School teachers. "We do know that her removal has planted another angel in Heaven."

TOMKIN CORRESPONDENT.

Lorna Doone by R. D. Blackmore presented to Alice Mary Docksey in 1928
Alice Docksey of Moor Hall Farm, died November 24th 1930 aged 14yrs.
The above article appeared in the local press at the time.

Annie, Arthur, Frederick and Ada Willshaw circa 1920's

Annie Baggaley (nee Willshaw) remembers being in the choir with her sister Ada, along with Mrs Beatie Bloor, Lily Hollinshead, Albert and Alice Docksey (brother and sister) Mr and Mrs Doolan, Mary and William Perkins (brother and sister), May Leech, Elsie Swindells, Mr Marson played the organ and Mrs Marson conducted the choir.

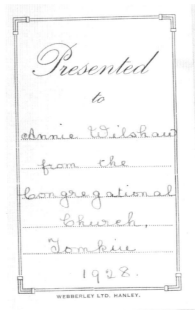

What Katy Did Next by Susan Coolidge presented to Annie Wilshaw in 1928.

82

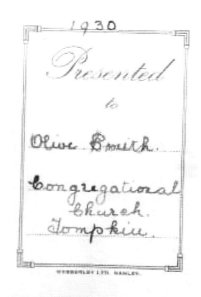 

What Katy Did by Susan Coolidge - presented to Olive Smith 1930. Olive pictured with her niece Joan Smith. Olive, of Lee House Farm, Cheddleton, died in 1936.

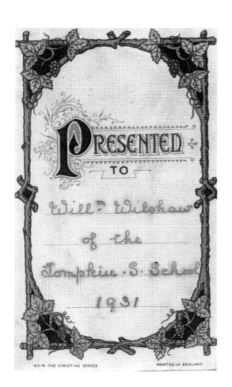 

Twinkle-tail stories Z.A.R. Nesbit - presented to William (Billy) Willshaw in 1931. William of Rosebank Farm, Cheddleton died in 1932, aged 7.

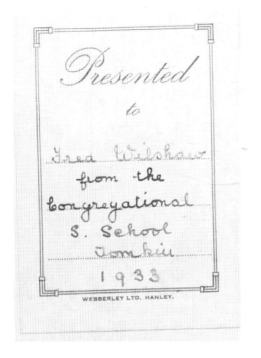

The Head boy at Bentley's - presented to Frederick C Willshaw 1933.
Fred attended Tomkin Sunday School between 1927-1934.
Fred has lived in Cheddleton all his life, he retired from farming at Rose Bank in 1971 and has since returned to attend services at Tomkin Chapel.

Ragged Robin by Katharine L. Oldmeadow -presented to Wilfred Edge 1934

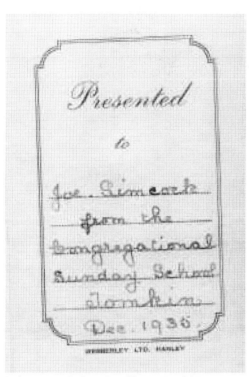

Prize awarded to Joe Simcock 1935

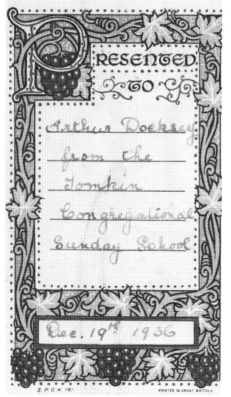

The Manor School by H Elrington- presented to Arthur Docksey from Moor Hall Farm in 1936. Arthur has lived and farmed all his life in the local area.

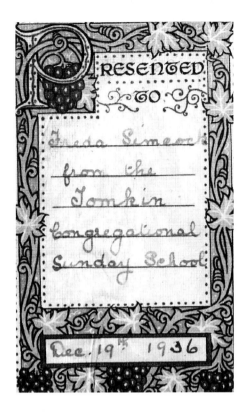

Freda Simcock

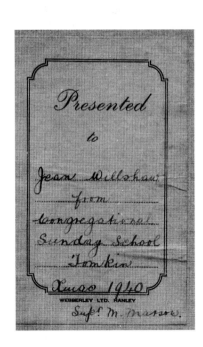

Wise and Witty Stories for Boys and Girls by Uncle Reg-presented to Jean Willshaw, by Superintendent M.Marson, Tomkin Sunday School, 1940. Photograph of Jean Willshaw at Lee House, Cheddleton.

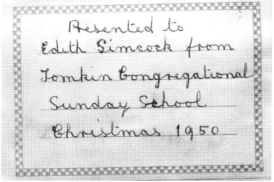

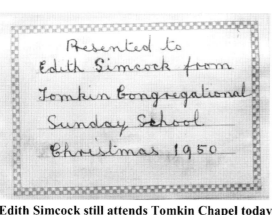

Edith Simcock still attends Tomkin Chapel today.

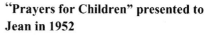

"Prayers for Children" presented to Jean in 1952

Jean Findlow started to attend Tomkin Chapel when she was 3. Mrs Marson used to collect her from her home at Knowsley Farm, and take her back after the service. Jean in later life helped with fund raising and the running of the Chapel along with Helen Bailey and Cynthia Brammer.

Chapter Fourteen

Chapel Exterior and Interior

Tomkin Chapel 2000

Stained glass window

Pulpit dressed for Harvest 1998

Christmas Fair 2001

Easter Flowers 2002 (left side of Chapel)

Easter 2002 (right side of Chapel)

Front view with stained glass window (Easter 2003)

Communion table cloth made by Joan Willshaw – lace edge donated by Elizabeth A. Willshaw of Hillside Road and formerly of Lee House, Cheddleton (lace estimated to be over 100 years old). Chairs from another Chapel and recovered for use at Tomkin.

Baptismal jug and bowl

The original tiny wooden font was stolen so the jug and bowl was made for the Chapel.

Jeff Harvey made the pen and ink sketch transfer of the chapel which was then added to the jug and bowl. Mary Allsopp, a retired gilder from Royal Doulton, gilded the rims and handle.

Chapter Fifteen

Personal Memories

Memories/notes by the late Henry Gordon Landon

Henry G Landon was born in 1908 the son of Archibald and Mary Landon. Henry Landon wrote the following (date when written unknown).

"It is known that Reverend R Newland minister of the Tabernacle, who helped to establish the Burslem Church in 1830, rode out to Tomkin on horseback. Ever since the worship at Tomkin started it as been led by lay preachers, mainly from Hanley in the first place.

Up to about 1925, lay preachers took the train from Stoke or Bucknall to Stockton Brook, and walked the rest; since then buses were more convenient until the car took over.

I remember as a boy walking with my father from Stockton Brook with snow up to my waist for a congregation of two. The congregation is gathered from one for two neighbouring cottages and farms within a two mile radius. Up to 15 years ago one could expect about a dozen adults and as many children. A few years ago electricity was installed, but I miss the old oil lamp and the Secretary getting up halfway through the sermon to put a couple of shovels full in the centrally situated stove."

Memories - David Landon

Tomkin used to be referred to as the little chapel in the Moorlands. My Father and I used to have tea with the Marsons back in the 1930's. I was only 12 or 13 at the time. We used to take the bus to Cheddleton and have tea with the Marsons and then walk to Tomkin Chapel. I'm pretty sure it was an evening service at that time, I can remember walking at night. I remember Mr Marson as a grey haired gentleman with moustache and a big voice.

Mr Marson always played the organ/harmonium, I'm told he taught himself. In so far as I can remember the Congregation attendance was quite good usually half to three quarters full.

My father Archibald Landon (Archie) carried on preaching and attending services until he was quite old even attending during very severe weather, we had a hard job persuading him not to go.

My Uncle Laurie Landon, (Lawrence) used to preacher at Tomkin as well, at the same period of time, he was a bit younger than my father.

Memories - Mrs Nora Landon (nee Wilde)

I went to Tomkin Chapel with Archie Landon, David's father, before we married. David and I never went together; David was away serving in the War. My husband's father (Archibald Landon) was one of the Lay Preachers from Hanley Tabernacle Congregational Church who used to take services regularly at Tomkin.

I was Nora Wilde then. Archie Landon and I used to go to Bagnall or Stanley on the bus and walk to the afternoon service which was timed to fit in with afternoon milking of the cows and with it being during the war to avoid the Blackout. Mr Landon used to call it "My Sunday at Tomkin".

There was a big stove in the middle of the Chapel; Mr Marson used to get off his organ seat and go and put on some coal. Even if the Minister was half way through his sermon he still got up and put some coal on.

Mr Marson invited us to tea; we would walk from Tomkin to Heath House for tea and catch the bus back to Hanley. Tomkin has always had a special place in our hearts.

Mrs Nora Landon (nee Wilde) April 1938
Outside Tomkin Chapel

The very first time I went to Tomkin, I thought I would be with these older people and I didn't know whether I should be able to contribute anything to the conversation so I decided to take my knitting with me. We walked from the Chapel to Heath House and when we got to the house, Mrs Marson said to sit down, and she got tea ready. The table appeared to be set and she seemed to be bringing things in for tea, and she appeared to be getting on with it, so I got my knitting out and started to knit. Mrs Marson came into the sitting room from the kitchen and said "what do you think you're doing" and I replied "well I've brought my knitting with me Mrs Marson" Mrs Marson replied " you're knitting on a Sunday, put it away and come and cut the bread and butter". I never forgot that incident. A time when such things were not allowed.

Memories – Arthur Docksey

When I was about 7 years of age, I recall that Lane End Farm was a corner shop for a little while; it sold allsorts and was open all hours. It was run by the Hardman's who came from Lancashire, they didn't stay long and went back to Lancashire before the war started.

I remember the Anniversary tea celebrations, and having games in the local fields.

I also remember the annual Christmas concert and prize giving. We all had to get involved and do something, whether it was to recite something or even do a play. I particularly remember Doreen Winkle and Hilda Gibson (now Goodwin) doing a play called "The Washerwoman", it would have been about 1936 or 37.

When I was about 10 or 12 years old, I noticed that the Sunday School attendance book was under the pulpit, and remember looking at it, one particular entry stuck in my mind, that of William Perkin (Jnr) it was for the period 1900-10.

If a Scholar had died during the year the other scholars were given a little black ribbon to fasten to their clothing. Mrs Marson gave these out has they lined up outside before entering to go on stage.

Memories - Joan Willshaw (nee Smith)

When I was born we lived at Lee House Farm, Cheddleton, we lived at one end of the house and my father's parents and my father's sister Olive lived at the other end.

Aunt Olive went to Sunday School at Tomkin Chapel. When I was 3 years old I was allowed to go with her. We walked across the fields to Black Bank Farm, and there we met up with my cousins Jean and George Willshaw and we walked together to the Chapel. I cannot remember if we met up with other children on the way. When we got to the little farm above the Chapel, the home of Mr and Mrs Banks, a dog always came out barking at us and I remember being very scared of this dog.

I enjoyed going to the Sunday School and can remember learning the hymns, particularly "Tell me the old old story" and "Tell me the stories of Jesus".

Sadly my Aunt Olive was taken ill and died in March 1936, she was only 14. The family were very upset and became unsettled so Grandad got another farm and we moved away to Woodhead Farm in Milton.

Memories - Jean Turner (nee Willshaw)

I used to walk from Lee House Farm to Rosebank Farm to take eggs to my Grandparents, and then meet Mr and Mrs Marson at the top of Coalpitford Lane, we would then walk across Knowsley Common to Tomkin for the afternoon service.

My Aunt, Ada Salmon, used to attend the special services at Tomkin, and I remember that when the service was over we would walk back together so far; she would turn off towards Long Shutes Farm at Thorney Edge and I went on to Rosebank Farm.

I remember quite a few other people who attended, Mrs Simcock with Joe, Freda, Joan, Edith, Mrs Mills, Mrs Bailey, Mrs Sylvester and her 3 sons, Mrs Landon, and Tommy Charlesworth to name a few.

I remember standing on the stage, no doubt like many others, but one occasion particularly sticks in my mind, it was so hot that I nearly fainted and had to be lifted off!

I also remember an Anniversary Tea, I would have been about 12-14, all the pews were moved and out came the trestle tables, and laden with a lovely spread of sandwiches and cakes. We also had running races/games in Docksey's field, the only flat field nearby.

Memories – Peter Handley

Tomkin Chapel was the centre of Tomkin village life.

My Grandfather Peter Handley used to run Tomkin Chapel at the beginning of the 1900's (1905-1914) he also used to play the organ. He farmed at Whistonshaw farm in Cheddleton.

I was born in 1933 and we moved from Whistonshaw to Burslem and soon after to Armshead. I attended Bagnall School at 9yrs old and became pally with Tommy Charlesworth. I used to cycle from Armshead to Tomkin to attend services.

When we were kids Mr and Mrs Marson were in charge. I remember sitting on the stage with my friend Tommy Charlesworth. The stage was made of rough cut oak boards which were held together with wrought iron rods, the rods were probably made at the Smithy. The stage was assembled when needed, and its construction enabled children to sit at different levels.

My sisters Dora, Hilda and Annie were all involved with the Chapel.

One of the stories my Father used to talk about was the arrival of a new harmonium; it was delivered to Endon Station and my father Fred collected it and took it to the chapel by horse and cart.

Memories – Tommy Charlesworth

I've lived at Far Rownall Farm all my life, I attended Bagnall School and I also used to attend Tomkin Chapel as a young lad; this was at a time when things were a lot different by today's standards. I used to look forward to going to Chapel every week. I never missed much, even attending during bad weather. My parents used to go occasionally particularly for special services. I remember the Marson's, they ran the Chapel including undertaking the services. I remember Jean and George Willshaw attending, the Simcock sisters, Freda, Edith and Joan, Mrs Landon and family, Albert and Eric Docksey, and Sheila Cornes to name a few.

Memories - Mary Allsopp

I remember having some nice times at the Chapel. After my sister Helen married Jim in 1965 she attended on a regular basis with her Mother-in-law Mrs Bailey. It was run by Mrs Riley at this time.

Mrs Bailey (Snr) first attended the Chapel in 1944. At this time Mr and Mrs Marson were running the Chapel, they asked Mrs Bailey if she would come regularly, and she said she would. Mr Marson was so pleased when she became a member that he threw his hat into the air. Mrs Bailey never missed a service till her death in 1984.

Mrs Bailey (Snr) came down from the farm and asked myself and my mother to join the Chapel. My Mother attended quite regularly and at first I went occasionally particularly for Harvest and Christmas services. Miss Proctor who lived in the cottage next to Mrs Riley at the Smithy also attended on a regular basis.

Mrs Riley moved to the Endon in the 1964 but still attended the Chapel until 1975. In 1975 Helen Bailey took over the running of the Chapel and it was at this time I became a regular member. Cynthia Brammer joined the Chapel in 1982 and helped Helen and Jean McNicol in running it together they decided to raise funds to renovate the Chapel and with the help of the Manpower Services Commission work started on the Chapel in 1984. The three worked really hard and achieved such a lot.

Many people used to help the Chapel in different ways. If we hadn't had the support of lay preachers it would not have continued for as long as it did. Pam Beech, a Lay Preacher from Burslem United Reformed Church, Clive Parsons, from Longton United Reformed Church gave us a lot of help. Mr Brayford used to do the annual Harvest auction. Eric Docksey attended the Chapel and played the organ. Mr and Mrs Kelsall who came from the Baptist Church at Baddeley Green often helped Helen organise trips etc and other events at the Chapel. Gillian Bailey and Brenda McNicol also helped with the stalls and fund raising. Gillian Bailey did a tracing of the stained glass window to form a pattern for a new pulpit cloth which I made and is still in the Chapel today. Gillian went on to become a designer once working for Woods and Son, Burslem and now for Churchill's.

We had Christmas nativity plays. I remember one year the stars of the nativity were Rosemary and Joan Steele, Brenda and Keith McNicol, Wain Eardley, John Bailey, Graham and Robert Hall.

Mr and Mrs Kelsall died and attendance fell even lower, so services went to once a month. By 1990 there were only 4 members left, Helen Bailey, Jean McNicol, John Bailey and myself.

Edward Bailey, my nephew was christened at the Chapel and Mrs Murphy from Lane End Farm had her funeral service there, she never attended services but supported the Chapel in other ways.

Memories of Jim Bailey of Tomkin Head Farm

Tomkin is in two parishes. The parish boundary marker is in the North East corner of the field which joins the Homestead. The marker which lies flat, was positioned to indicate where the 3 parishes join together, Bagnall, Cheddleton and Stanley. The farm originally had one field in Bagnall all the rest in Cheddleton.

My parents married in 1938 and came to Tomkin Head Farm at that time. The previous tenants had been the Edge family. At first they rented the farm like many others did and after a few years they bought it from the owner. The farm was originally 58 acres.

The barn has a date on it of 1826, so the original farmhouse could have been of a similar date. The old farmhouse was originally built of stone. It was an extremely damp house, my parents lived in one of the rooms downstairs and one up, where the fire grates were, it was so damp even the wallpaper wouldn't stick to the walls.

My father was quite successful as a dairy farmer; he could afford to build a new house. This was at a time when damp proofing etc didn't exist so the old stone building was knocked down and a new house built in 1953.

My parents and myself outside Tomkin Head Farm Circa 1949 – in front of the original stone built farmhouse.

The house next door (Grange View) was built in 1965 when Helen and I married.

I attended Tomkin Chapel from about the age of 3 or 4, before I started school. I attended quite regularly, but as I got older I went less frequent. My Mother attended for 40 years.

I remember Mrs Sneyd who used to attend Chapel when my mother used to go. The Sneyd's lived down the road, half way in between Tomkin and Stanley. Mr Sneyd used to go to the pub in Stanley Village and play the piano. We needed an organist so Mr Sneyd volunteered for a short period of time; he wasn't a church goer as such.

Mr Sneyd had other talents including painting. I remember Mr Sneyd sitting opposite Tomkin Chapel on a number of occasions, painting the image before him. The painting, a watercolour of the chapel, was presented to the Mr and Mrs Marson when they left Tomkin. My mother used to visit Mrs Marson when she was in a nursing home in Uttoxeter and on one occasion Mrs Marson made a gift of the painting to her and we still have the painting today, and is signed "C V Sneyd".

Mr Sneyd died suddenly. Mrs Sneyd continued to attend Chapel for a while and then went to live with her daughter in Eastbourne.

Before the Riley's moved into the Smithy, Arthur Salt, his wife and his 3 sons lived there. They didn't attend Chapel. Arthur was a physically strong man, who had been a boxer at sometime in his past, who worked in the Potteries, and also farmed his 12 acres at Tomkin. He was known to do a days work and then come home to mow his field at night with a scythe! He moved and went to work at Cheddleton Paper Mill, and on one occasion was pulled into the machinery, and it is said that the reason he survived was total due to his physical strength.

Mr and Mrs Riley came to Tomkin Smithy in the 1940's. The Smithy with 12 acres was owned by a Mr Cundy. Initially the Riley's rented it from Mr Cundy and then bought it the following year. There was a family connection between the Riley's and Cundy's.

Miss Proctor, Mrs Riley's sister, moved to Tomkin in 1954 to live in the Cottage next to the Smithy. Miss Proctor also attended Chapel with her sister on a regular basis.

The Riley's moved to Endon in 1964, but this didn't stop Mrs Riley, she continued to run the chapel and did so until she died suddenly in 1975. Mr and Mrs Riley and Miss Proctor are buried at Longnor. After this the Chapel was run for a very short time by a young man named Geoffrey Hine. He had the fire removed which so many remember being in the middle of the chapel and installed new electric heaters.

We had ministerial support from the Congregational Church in Leek and Lay Preachers came from the Potteries. The Reverend Appleby in the 1950's, Reverend Booth and finally Reverend Farrar in the 1970's all came from Leek and they probably came once a month for Communion services. Tomkin Chapel was under the mother Church of Leek until the Staffordshire Congregational Union amalgamated and became part of the United Reformed Church.

The Reverend Farrar called a meeting in 1975 and wanted to close Tomkin Chapel as only 3 or 4 were now attending. It was at this stage that Jean McNicol and my wife Helen Bailey took it over to prevent this happening. The Reverend Farrar continued to take services at Tomkin until he retired in the 1980's. After this Ministers came from Burslem.

Tomkin Head Cottage

Tomkin Head Cottage in the distance, The Smithy and Chapel hidden by the trees and bushes

The cottage was a one up, one down building with a kitchen at the back and came with 6 acres. The access to it was through the Smithy entrance.

Mr Worthington lived here at the Cottage between the 1940's-1950's, and then Ken Ball and family. By 1954 Miss Proctor had arrived and lived here for 10 years until 1964. When Mrs Riley moved to Endon, her sister Miss Proctor decided to move at the same time, and moved to Leek in 1964.

The Riley's sold the Smithy to Mr Whilock and the land to me, and Miss Proctor sold the cottage to Mr Allsopp and the land to me. The Smithy land is in Bagnall and Tomkin Head Cottage land in Cheddleton, the boundary followed a dividing wall between the land. So now the total land size of Tomkin Head Farm is 76 acres.

The cottage was rented to a number of people after Miss Proctor left, Mr and Mrs Rogers, Jean and Norman McNicol, but the cottage became uninhabitable and eventually fell down. With this property being derelict the Allsopp family from Bagnall Grange obtained planning permission to build a new property, a bungalow, on another piece of land which is located just below the Chapel. The Allsopp family still own the plot of land where the cottage stood today.

Lane End Farm

I remember my parents telling me that 3 people lived there named Leech; May Leech, her Mother and an elderly gentleman relation. They moved to Alstonefield but remained the owners of Lane End Farm renting the property out to various families. May then married a man named Davidson. (George Davidson 1935).

The Landon family lived at Lane End from the 1940's and then moved roughly the same time as I got married, 1964-65. There was Charlie, Lydia and five children.

Then the Murphy family moved in. When Mrs Murphy died the service was held at Tomkin Chapel. Mr Murphy is still living today.

The Murphy and Landon families rented Lane End Farm from Mrs M Davidson (nee Leech), who used to live at the property before her marriage. The property was only sold about 14/15 years ago when Mr Murphy left.

Lane End Farm Circa 1930

Memories – Cynthia Brammer

It was just before Christmas 1981 when we first saw the "FOR SALE" sign go up on The Smithy at Tomkin. For nine years Gilbert and I had been living in the villas at Hallwater in Endon, travelling up the bank to the farm on Thorney Edge everyday to work. Buying a country cottage was difficult as price rises made it hard to afford the move, but we took the opportunity to view it quickly. We liked what we saw and put an offer in straight away. Then we waited and waited, till May to be precise. Still the "For Sale" sign stayed up and we assumed that someone else had got it. Then one day my Father-in-law dropped into the estate agent and asked why the SOLD sign had not gone up and was told that the people who had made the highest offer could not sell their own home and the sale was now getting more urgent. So we renewed our offer and were delighted when it was accepted. Less than six weeks later, after much sorting and packing moved us and the children to Tomkin 26 June 1982.

On one of the first Sundays we noticed the folk walking down the lane, and realised the Chapel must have a service on, so myself and the children, then 7, 5 and 3 got ready quickly and joined them. It was an introduction to meet some of the local folk and visiting Lay Preachers that we have since grown to know well over the years.

There wasn't too many people going then, the Harvest Service was the main event and drew people back, year on year; it was this feeling of belonging that kept the small Chapel alive. The Lay Preachers were strong in their support and as more children began to appear a Thursday Club started for the younger ones and six teenagers were taught their commitments and became Church Members, under the guidance of Pam Beech. Those seeds sown in those early years are now bearing fruit for the future of the Chapel as a new generation are being baptised and learning their Christian roots in the Chapel as did their Mums' before them.

But wait; step back a little to the 1980's. During those first few years as we met and talked, we realised that jobs needed doing just to keep it in good order. First of all the spouting was leaking, water running down the outer walls and making it damp. So he had a coffee morning at The Smithy and later around Harvest time we held a meat and potato pie supper there too. Lots came and jobs were started.

We were lucky that in the 1990's a scheme started which was sponsored by the City; where people out of work were trained in new skills. The scheme was looking for projects to undertake and accepted ours. So with their team of free labour, our costs were for materials only. We were able to have a new roof and floor and the outer walls were re-rendered and all of the wood lining inside was renewed too. The beams and pews were treated and we were able to replace the pulpit, chairs and table and add a small font when the Chapel at Great Haywood closed. The communion rail came from the little church at Kingsley Moor. The new cross above the communion table was made by the joiner from the wood from a pew from May Bank Chapel when it too closed. Also the harmonium, which had a tendency to lose its wind mid service, gave up altogether, we managed to buy a new keyboard; unfortunately it later stolen along with our small font, when the Chapel had a break in.

During the time of refurbishment the services were held at the now closed, St Agnes Mission in Stanley, just opposite the Travellers Rest and the Harvest Service was held at Endon Chapel; a marvellous cooperation between the local churches.

When the work was completed, we had a lovely service of rededication. It was a time of working together and pleasure. The children too grew closer and their families. At Christmas time each year they would come together on a couple of evenings and go carolling round the farms and cottages. One rather special memory was our start at Moor Hall, about 6.30pm when Albert, Arthur and Steve were milking cows. We would all stand at the end of the byre and sing and they would join us. Albert always said the milk was plentiful on that particular evening; so the animals must have enjoyed it too!

A few years' later numbers decreased and the remaining members decided to close.

It was at this time that the community came together again and with the guidance and blessing of the United Reformed Church, led by the Rev. Kevin Jones, Rev. Ivor Davies, and Rev.Barry Griffin, along with Mr John Davey from Uttoxeter, Mr Maurice Williams from Wolstanton and Mr Geoff Harrison and Rachel Greening from District. On December 17th 1997, the doors opened again for the Christmas Service, the people came and they filled the Chapel, some expected, some not, some we knew, and some we didn't.

It was the beginning of our small hilltop Chapel's NEW LIFE. The coming together of a new flock of people; the developing of a new structure; where the Ministers provided their knowledge and guidance; where church meetings took place; where all could have a voice. The feeling of hope, with new community outreach events, like our open weekends at Easter, barbeques in summer, and our shared walks and meetings and events with other churches at Longton and Uttoxeter.

Even now things change and grow, with our new Tuesday Morning "Tea and Chat", once a month, which brings in folk who don't as a rule attend services, but like so many people nowadays they are not used to being brought up in a Church environment with faith and support around them, but are finding their way to us and us to them.

The one thing that has struck me forcibly during my comparatively short time on the hill at Tomkin is the feeling of belonging and the will to keep the little Chapel in their lives and for generations to come.

Appendices

Families listed as living at Tomkin 1841

1841	Census	Bagnall Parish	Tompkin
William	**Salt**	Age 30	Farmer
Ann	**Salt**	Age 25	
Samuel	**Wood**	Age 25	Blacksmith
Elizabeth	**Wood**	Age 25	
Harriet	**Wood**	Age 6	
Ann?	**Wood**	Age 1	
Female	**?**	?	
Mary	**Wood**	Age 35	
Ellen	**Wood**	Aged 6	Part of entry unable to
Ellen	**?**	Aged 20	decipher
Ralph	**Knight**	Age 40	Agricultural
Ann	**Knight**	Age 35	Labourer
Frances	**Knight**	Daughter Age 3	
James	**Knight**	8 Months?	
William	**?**	Aged 7	
Mary	**Greaves**	Aged 35	
John	**Greaves**	Aged 1 Month	
Moor Hall			
Hugh	**Ford**	Aged 50	Farmer
Ellen	**Heath**	Aged 35	Farmer
Catherine	**Heath**	Aged 15	
Female	**Steele**	Aged 15	Female Servant
James	**Allen**	Aged 25	Male Servant
John	**Allen**	Aged 20	Male Servant
William	**Mollert**	Aged 15	Male Servant
Samuel	**Simson**	Aged 20	Male Servant
B...?	**Ward**	Aged 20	Male Servant
Thomas	**Kirkham**	Aged 15	Male Servant

Some of the images from the 1841 Census are of very poor quality and very hard to decipher.
1841 also has less information than the following ones.

Families listed as living at Tomkin 1851

1851	Census	Bagnall Parish	Tompkin	Born
Tompkin				
William	**Brooks**	Married Age 29	Farmer of 13 acres and Ag. Labourer	Stoke-on-Trent
Hannah	**Brooks**	Wife Age 22		Cheddleton
Phoeby	**Brooks**	Daughter Aged 3		Leek
William	**Brooks**	Son Aged 6 months		Stoke-on-Trent
Tompkin				
Thomas	**Heath**	Unmarried Age 20	Farmer of 85 acres employing 1 indoor and 1 outdoor servant	Caverswall
Mary	**Heath**	Sister/unmarr/Aged 22	Housekeeper	Caverswall
David	**Pegg**	Servt/unmarried/Age 22	Ag. Labourer	Leek
Tompkin				
Samuel	**Wood**	Married Aged 39	Farmer of 10 acres & Mst Blacksmith Employing 1 man	Biddulph
Elizabeth	**Wood**	Wife 39		Macclesfield
Samuel G.	**Wood**	Son Aged 5	Scholar	S.O.T.
James	**Wood**	Son Aged 3		S.O.T.
James	**Kennedy? or Kennerly**	Apprentice Aged 16	Blacksmiths Apprentice	Eaton Cheshire
Moor Hall				
Ellen	**Heath**	Widow Aged 49	Landed Proprietor	Norton in the Moors
Ellen	**Simcock**	Married Daughter Aged 30		S.O.T.
Elizabeth	**Simcock**	Visitor Aged 3		Cheddleton

Families listed as living at Tomkin 1861

1861	Census	Bagnall Parish	Tomkin	Born
Springfield, Tomkin				
Samuel	**Wood**	Married Aged 49	Blacksmith &	Biddulph
Elizabeth	**Wood**	Wife 49	Farmer of 11 acres	Macclesfield
Samuel G.	**Wood**	Son Aged 15	Timber Merchant	S.O.T.
James	**Wood**	Son Aged 13	Scholar	S.O.T.
John	**Bainbridge**	Apprentice Aged 19 (unmarried)	Blacksmiths Apprentice	Cheddleton
Tomkin Chapel Independent (Brief mention)				
Tomkin				
Ellen	**Heath**	Widow Aged 59	Farmer of 73 acres	Norton
Ann	**Heath**	Daug.Aged 32 single	Farmers Daughter	Caverswall
Thomas	**Heath**	Son Aged 29 single	Farmers son	Caverswall
Thomas	**Ford**	Brother Aged 63	Retired Farmer	Norton
Emma	**Shaw**	Servant Aged 13	General Servant	Caverswall
Richard	**Forrester**	Servant Aged 28 Single	Carter	Hanley
Elijah	**Hill**	Servant Aged 23 Single	Cowman	Stoke
Little Tomkin				
Martha	**Billinge**	Widow Aged 35	School Mistress	Hanley
Sarah	**Billinge**	Daughter Aged 9	Scholar	Leek
Charlotte	**Billinge**	Daughter Aged 7	Scholar	S.O.T.
Elizabeth	**Billinge**	Daughter Aged 3	Scholar	S.O.T.
Moor Hall				
Samuel	**Fenton**	Married Aged 61	Farmer of 127 acres	S.O.T.
Julia	**Fenton**	Wife Aged 57		S.O.T.
Sarah	**Fenton**	Daughter Aged 31		S.O.T.
Ralph	**Fenton**	Son Aged 26		Burlsem
Ephraim	**Fenton**	Son Aged 22		Burslem
Harriet	**Fenton**	Daughter Aged 16		Burslem
Alice	**Fenton**	Daughter Aged 13	Dress Maker	Burslem
William	**Washington**	Servant Aged 19	Cowman	Cheddleton
Nathan	**Jackson**	Servant Aged 14	Ploughman	Cheddleton

Families listed as living at Tomkin 1871

1871	Census	Bagnall Parish	Tomkin	Born
James	**Wood**	Married Aged 24	Blacksmith & Farmer of 11 acres employing 1 man	S.O.T.
Jane	**Wood**	Wife Aged 23	...	Chester, Withington
Annie Elizabeth	**Wood**	Daughter Aged 4	...	S.O.T.
Arthur	**Wood**	Son Aged 3	...	S.O.T.
Walter	**Wood**	Son Aged 2	...	S.O.T.
Elizabeth	**Wood**	Mother (Widow) Aged 59	...	Macclesfield
Ralph Finney	**Johnson**	Apprentice Aged 17	Blacksmith Apprentice	Leek
Ralph	**Alcock**	Married Aged 49	Farmer 57 acres	Onecote
Olive	**Alcock**	Wife Aged 51	Farmers wife	Cheddleton
Harriet	**Alcock**	Unmarried Aged 21	Farmers daughter	Leek
Thomas	**Alcock**	Unmarried Aged 18	Farmers son	Leek
Mary	**Alcock**	Unmarried Aged 16	Farmers daughter	Leek
Harriet	**Bridgwood**	Niece Aged 5	Scholar	S.O.T.
Joseph	**James**	Married Aged 56	Coal Miner	Kinglsey
Sarah	**James**	Wife Aged56		Kingsley
Ellis	**Rowith**	Visitor Aged 65 Unmarried	No Occupation	S.O.T.
John	**Sherratt**	Married Aged 68	Farmer of 126 acres	Congleton, Cheshire
Eve	**Sherratt**	Wife Aged 69		Biddulph
John	**Sherratt**	Unmarried Aged 43	Farmers son	Horton
Josiah	**Sherratt**	Unmarried Aged 35	Farmers son	Astbury, Chs
James	**Sherratt**	Married Aged 33	Farmers son	Astbury, Chs
Emily	**Sherratt**	Daughter-in-law Aged 21	...	S.O.T.
Ann	**Sherratt**	Grddaughter Aged 3 wks	....	S.O.T.
Selina	**Heath**	Servant Aged 15	General domestic	Cheddleton

Families listed as living at Tomskin 1881

1881	Census	Bagnall Parish	Tomskin	Born
William	**Deakin**	Married Aged 31	Farmer 12 Acres &	Leek
Fanny	**Deakin**	Married Aged 31	Blacksmith	Ipstones
William	**Deakin**	Son Aged 3	Potters apprentice	S.O.T.
William	**Beech**	Visitor Aged 13	Blacksmiths	S.O.T.
George	**Hoyland**	Unmarried Aged 18	Apprentice	Ipstones
		TOMSKIN CHAPEL		
Tomskin Lane Head?				
Ralph	**Alcock**	Married Aged 59	Farmer 50 acres	Onecote
Olive	**Alcock**	Wife Aged 61	employing 1 labourer	Cheddleton
Mary	**Alcock**	Unmarried Aged 26	Farmers daughter	Leek
Harriett	**Bridgwood**	Niece Aged 15		Hanley
Little Tomskin				
Tm. Henry	**Durose**	Married Aged 33	Farmer / Labourer	London Sitty*
Sarah Sadler	**Durose**	Wife Aged 35	3acres	Bonbury, Cheshire
Ann	**Chatfied**	Mother/widow Aged 63		Uttoxeter
Moor Hall				
Daniel	**Steele**	Unmarried Aged 41	Farmer of 130 acres	S.O.T.
Sarah	**Steele**	Sister unmarried Aged 44	Housekeeper	S.O.T.
Ephraim	**Steele**	Brother Married Aged 43	Publican out of	S.O.T.
Sarah	**Steele**	Sister in law Aged 40	(business?) Wife	Widness, Lanc
Mary Gertrude	**Steele**	Niece Aged 3	Daughter Aged 3	Wales
George	**Broadhurst**	Servant Aged 14	Farm Servant	Newcastle

*Spelt has appears in the Census

Families listed as living at Tomkin 1891

1891	Census	Bagnall Parish	Tomskin	Born
Tomskin				
William	**Deakin**	Married Aged 41	Blacksmith	Cheddleton
Fanny	**Deakin**	Wife Aged 41		Ipstones
Wm	**Deakin**	Son Aged 13	Scholar	Bagnall
Eliz	**Deakin**	Daughter Aged 9	Scholar	Bagnall
George	**Deakin**	Son Aged 6	Scholar	Bagnall
Annie	**Deakin**	Daughter Aged 6	Scholar	Bagnall
Tomskin				
Wm	**Chell**	Married Aged 36	Farmer	Basford Grange
Ellen	**Chell**	Wife Aged 35		Basford
Minnie	**Chell**	Daughter Aged 10	Scholar	Basford
George	**Chell**	Son Aged 7	Scholar	Basford
Annie	**Chell**	Daughter Aged 5		Tomskin
Wm	**Chell**	Son Aged 3		Tomskin
Lizzie	**Chell**	Daughter Aged 1		Tomskin
Fanny	**Chell**	Daughter Aged 5 weeks		Tomskin
Little Tomskin				
Isaac	**Simcock**	Married Aged 50	Farmer	Horton
Annie	**Simcock**	Wife Aged 51		Horton
Moor Hall				
Daniel	**Steel**	Unmarried Aged 50	Farmer	Eaves Lane
Sarah	**Steel**	Unmarried Sister Aged 53		Eaves Lane
Mary	**Steel**	Mother Aged 77		Small Brook
George	**Bank**	Servant Unmarried Aged 21	Ag Servant	Baddeley Edge

Families listed as living at Tomkin 1901

1901	Census	Bagnall Parish	Tomkin	Born
Tomkin				
Joseph	**Shenton**	Married Aged 29	Forge Labourer	Withy Stakes
Eliza	**Shenton**	Wife Aged 27		Baddeley Edge
Elsie?	**Shenton**	Daughter Aged 4		Tomkin
Elizabeth	**Shenton**	Daughter Aged 2		Tomkin
Tomkin				
John	**Banks**	**Married Aged 60**	Forge Labourer	Clayton
May	**Banks**	**Wife Aged 61**		Armshead
End of Ecclesiastical Parish of St Edwards Cheddleton				
Tomkin				
James	**Myatt**	Married Aged 36	Farmer	Bagnall
Sarah	**Myatt**	Wife Aged 38		S.O.T.
George J	**Myatt**	Son Aged 4		Cheddleton
Charles E	**Myatt**	Son Aged 3		Cheddleton
John	**Myatt**	Son Aged 2		Cheddleton
Mary A	**Myatt**	Daughter Aged 11 Months		Tomkin
Richard W	**Murfin**	Servant Aged 17	Cowman	Bradnop
Eunice	**Salt**	Servant Aged 14	Domestic	Milton
Tomkin				
William	**Perkin**	Married Aged 34	Blacksmith	Kingsley
Sarah	**Perkin**	Wife Aged35		Hanley
Charles	**Perkin**	Son Aged 10		Kingsley
William	**Perkin**	Son Aged 8		Bucknall
Mabel	**Perkin**	Daughter Aged 4		Bucknall
Hilda	**Perkin**	Daughter Aged 5		Bucknall
May	**Perkin**	May Aged 1		Tomkin
Moor Hall				
Joshua	**Steele**	Married Aged 52	Farmer	Bagnall
Annie	**Steele**	Wife Aged 43		Butterton
Maud	**Steele**	Daughter Aged 13		Wetley Rocks
Joshua	**Steele**	Son Aged 13		Bagnall
Ecclesiastical Parish of Bucknall and Bagnall				

Bagnall Parish Registers

Baptisms 1813-1903 Tomkin and Moor Hall entries only

Date	Name	Parents names and	Surname	Place	Occupation
8 January 1815	William	George & Hannah	Martin	Moor Hall	Farmer
10 March 1816	Hannah	George & Hannah	Martin	Moor Hall	Farmer
5 October 1817	Eliza	George & Hannah	Martin	Moor Hall	Farmer
14 March 1819	Mary	George & Hannah	Martin	Moor Hall	Farmer
26 November 1820	Julia	George & Hannah	Martin	Moor Hall	Farmer
10 Jan 1821	Ellen	Thomas & Ellen	Heath	Tompkin	Farmer
12 May 1822	Lucy	George & Hannah	Martin	Moor Hall	Farmer
23 November 1823	Ann	George & Hannah	Martin	Moor Hall	Farmer
26 June 1825	Matilda	George & Hannah	Martin	Moor Hall	Farmer
19 August 1827	George	George & Hannah	Martin	Moor Hall	Farmer
12 June 1831	Alfred	Thomas & Anne	Basnett	Tomkin	Farmer
22 March 1835	Harriet	Samuel and Eliz	Wood	Tomkin	Blacksmith
17 May 1835	William	James & Mary	Davenport	Tompkin	Labourer
29 Jan 1837	Sarah Born	James & Mary 6 April 1833	Davenport	Tomkin	Labourer
4 Feb 1838	Eliza	James & Mary	Davenport	Tompkin	Labourer
22 Sept 1850	William Wood	William & Hannah	Brooks	Tomkin	Labourer
No more entries listed until 1877					
23 Dec 1877	Charles	James Wood & Harriet	Kirkam	Tomkin	Farmer
24 Nov 1878	Rosie Annie	Joshua & Annie	Steele	Knowsley Grange Tomkin	Farmer
2 Jun 1881	Ada	Thomas & Sarah	Durose	Tomkin	Labourer
21 June 1884	Annie	William & Fanny	Deakin	Tomkin	Blacksmith
21 June 1884	George	William & Fanny	Deakin	Tomkin	Blacksmith
22 Nov 1885	Annie	William & Ellen	Chell	Tomkin	Farmer
14 Aug 1887	William	William & Ellen	Chell	Tomkin	Farmer
19 May 1889	Lizzie	William & Ellen	Chell	Tomkin	Farmer
3 May 1891	Fanny	William & Ellen	Chell	Tomkin	Farmer
9 April 1893	Mary	William & Ellen	Chell	Tomkin	Farmer
29 Oct 1899	Lizzie	Willam & Annie	Hine	Tomkin	Farmer
20 May 1900	May	William & Ellen	Perkins	Tomkin	Blacksmith
22 Sept 1900	Mary Agnes	James & Sarah Ann	Myatt	Tomkin	Farmer
29 March 1903	William	James & Sarah Ann	Myatt	Tomkin	Farmer

Burials 1834-1900
2 entries only

Date	Name	Place	Age
11 November 1846	Samuel Heath	Moor Hall	2yrs
24 April 1870	Samuel Wood	Tomkin	58 yrs
19 March 1882	Nathan Jackson	Tomkin	63yrs

Marriages 1837-1925

Date	Names	Age	Occupation	Where living	Name of father	Occupation
1 June 1854	Robert Walley and Catherine Heath	26 30?	Farmer	Park Lane, Leek Tomkin	William Walley Thomas Heath	? Farmer
5 June 1900	William J M Oulsnam and Jessie Goodall	21? 26	?	Fenton Tomkin, Bagnall	William Oulsnam Charles Goodall	Farmer Farmer
11 June 1922	Percy Glover and Hilda Perkin	26 26	Fireman	Baddeley Edge Smithy, Tomkin	George Glover William Perkin	Manager Blacksmith

A large proportion of the entries in the marriage registers on microfiche between 1837-1914 are of very poor quality and therefore very hard to read, due to this one or two may have been missed.

Tomkin by Bette Wilson

A Chapel in the Moorlands
Where farming families pray
Built in the reign of Victoria
Special in so many ways
This place has a long history
Not so easy to find
Local people stayed loyal
But numbers went into decline

There's a story about
how it came by its name
A Civil War Drummer called "Tom"
I won't say much about this tale
It's not such a pleasant one.
I suppose it should really be "Tom's Skin"
Referring of course to his drum
Now it's just know as TOMKIN
A haven for all people who come.

The Chapel sadly closed for a while
Then at Christmas reopened in style
What could be better than Jesus' birth
For the faithful at Tomkin to show their true worth.
Neighbouring fellowship all rallied round
Things which were needed soon had been found
Once again God's praises were heard
Music, singing and hearing His Word.

Throughout this year Tomkin has thrived
The Country surrounding will come alive
Special events planned, services too
Now there'll be many not just a few
Remember all those who've prayed in this place
Remember all those who received God's Grace
Remember heartaches and happiness too
Give thanks to God for all who've stayed true.

Xmas Eve

One Xmas Eve when Santa Claus
Called at a certain house
To fill the Children's stockings
There he found a little mouse.
"A Merry Christmas, Little Friend"
Said Santa, good and kind.
"The same to you, Sir", said the mouse,
"I thought you would not mind
If I should stay awake tonight
And watch you for a while".
"Your are very welcome, Little Mouse",
Said Santa with a smile
Then he reached the stockings down
And before the mouse could wink
From top to toe, from top to toe,
There wasn't left a chink.
"Now they won't hold another thing"
Said Santa Claus with pride
The mouse, he chuckled to himself
And humbly he replied
"It's not polite to contradict,
Your pardon, I implore,
But in the fullest stocking there,
I could put one thing more"
"Oh, oh" laughed Santa, "Silly Mouse,
Don't I know how to pack?
Been filling stockings all these years,
I should have learnt the knack!"
And then he reached the stocking down
From where it hung so high
And said "Now put in one thing more,
I give you leave to try"
The mouse, he chuckled to himself
And then he softly stole
Right to the crowded stocking toe
And gnawed a little hole.
"Now, if you please, good Santa Claus,
I've put in one thing more.
For you will own, that little hole,
Was not in there before!"
How Santa Claus did laugh and laugh
And then he gaily spoke
"Well you shall have a Christmas cheese,
For that nice little joke!"

This Christmas poem was recited at Tomkin Chapel Christmas Concerts, around 80 to 100 years ago by Mr Alf Leese, from Leese's Wheelwrights, Scotia Road, Burslem. He was the brother of Mrs Perkin who lived at The Smithy.

Bibliography

Adams, Percy. History of the Adams family. 1914

Bagnall- On the fringe of the Moorlands. Ed. By Robert Speake. 1990

Chevalier de Johnstone. Memoirs of the rebellion in 1745 and 1746

Congregational Church, Burslem, 150th Anniversary Booklet 1821-1971

Duffy, Christopher. The '45 – Bonnie Prince Charlie and the untold story of the Jacobite rising

Electoral Registers 1902-1967

Greenslade, M. W. and Stuart, D.G. A History of Staffordshire.1965

Jamieson, W.M. Murders, Myths and Monuments of North Staffordshire

Matthews, A. G. The Congregational Churches of Staffordshire. London. 1924

Milner, Robert. (ed) Cheddleton. A Village History. 1983

Moxon, J.E. The History of Horton Hall. Churnet Valley Books. 1997

People of the Potteries: A Dictionary of Local Biography Vol. 1 Ed. By Denis Stuart. Department of Adult Education, University of Keele. 1985

Ray, James History of the Rebellion; from its rise in 1745 to its total suppression.(1754)

Shaw, Simeon. History of the Staffordshire Potteries.1829

Staffordshire Congregational Reports 1885-1967

Ward, John. History of the Borough of Stoke-upon-Trent. 1843

White, William. History, Gazetteer and Directory of Staffordshire. 1851